Algebra 2

Practice Workbook

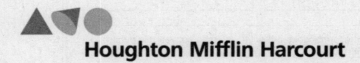

Houghton Mifflin Harcourt

Contents

Student Worksheets

Module 22   Gathering and Displaying Data

Module 23   Data Distributions

Module 24   Making Inferences from Data

Name _____ Date _____ Class _____

Domain, Range, and End Behavior
Practice and Problem Solving: A/B

Describe the interval shown using an inequality, set notation, and interval notation.

1.

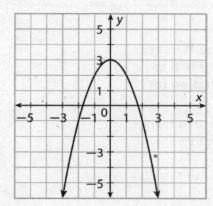

Inequality: _____

Set Notation: _____

Interval Notation: _____

2.

Inequality: _____

Set Notation: _____

Interval Notation: _____

Describe the domain and range of the graph using an inequality, set notation, and interval notation. Then describe its end behavior.

3. Graph of $f(x) = -x^2 + 3$:

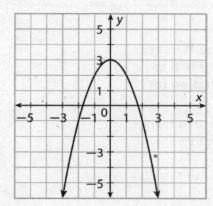

Domain:

Inequality: _____

Set Notation: _____

Interval Notation: _____

Range:

Inequality: _____

Set Notation: _____

Interval Notation: _____

End Behavior:

_____

Draw the graph of the function with its given domain. Then determine the range using interval notation.

4. $g(x) = -3x + 2$ with domain $(-1, 2]$:

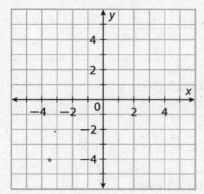

Range: _____

5. $h(x) = 0.5x - 1$ with domain $(-\infty, 4)$:

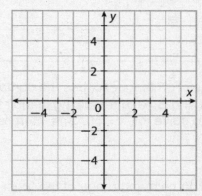

Range: _____

LESSON
1-1

Domain, Range, and End Behavior

Practice and Problem Solving: C

For Problems 1–2, let $f(x) = x^2 - 4$.

1. Graph the function.

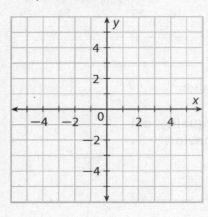

2. Determine the domain and range of f using set notation and interval notation. Then describe its end behavior.

_____

_____

_____

_____

Home A uses 8 gallons of propane per day for heat. Home B uses 5 gallons per day. Both homes begin with propane tanks filled to their maximum capacities of 500 gallons. Use this information for Problems 3–6.

3. Write two linear functions modeling the amount of propane remaining in each tank per day. Then graph both functions on the same coordinate plane.

   Home A: _____; Home B: _____

4. Describe the domain and range of each function using interval notation.

   _____

   _____

5. Write a function that describes the combined amount of propane Homes A and B have remaining in their tanks per day. Use the function to solve for $x = 50$, and interpret the result.

   _____

6. Write the domain and range of the function found in Problem 5 using set notation.

   _____

LESSON 1-2 Characteristics of Function Graphs

Practice and Problem Solving: A/B

Use the graph to answer Problems 1–4.

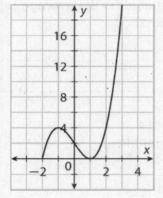

1. On which intervals is the function increasing and decreasing?

   _____

   _____

2. What are the local maximum and minimum values?

   _____

   _____

3. What are the zeros of the function?

   _____

4. What is the domain and range?

   _____

   _____

Shelley is studying the relationship between her car's mileage (miles per gallon) and speed (miles per hour). The table shows the data Shelley found. Use the table for Problems 5–7.

Speed (miles per hour)	30	40	50	60	70
Mileage (miles per gallon)	34.0	33.5	31.5	29.0	27.5

5. Make a scatter plot of the data. Then use a calculator to find an equation for the line of best fit. Sketch the line.

   Equation of line: _____

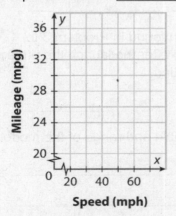

6. Use the equation found in Problem 5 to predict the miles per gallon of Shelly's car for a speed of 55 miles per hour.

   _____

7. Is the prediction found in Problem 6 an example of interpolation or extrapolation? Explain.

   _____

   _____

   _____

LESSON 1-2 Characteristics of Function Graphs

Practice and Problem Solving: C

The table shows values of a polynomial function. Use the table for Problems 1–2.

x	0	1	2	3
f(x)	20	15	12	41

1. Over which intervals is the average rate of change positive?

   _____

   _____

2. Over which intervals is the average rate of change negative?

   _____

   _____

A fireworks projectile is launched at 20 meters per second from a 60-meter cliff. The table shows the height, *y*, in meters the projectile is above a field after *x* seconds. Use the table for Problems 3–9.

Time (seconds)	0	1	2	3	4	5
Height (meters)	60	75	80	75	60	35

3. Make a scatter plot of the data. Then use the QuadReg feature on a calculator to find a function that best fits the data. Sketch the function.

   Function: _____

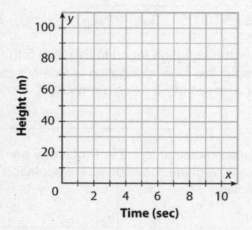

4. What is the maximum height of the projectile? _____

5. Over what interval is the projectile's height increasing? _____

6. Over what interval is the projectile's height decreasing? _____

7. Use the equation found in Problem 3 to find the height after 7 seconds. Does this prediction make sense for the problem situation? Explain.

   _____

   _____

8. Use the equation found in Problem 3 to predict how long after the launch the projectile reaches the ground.

   _____

9. What is the domain and range of the model?

   _____

   _____

LESSON 1-3

Transformations of Function Graphs

Practice and Problem Solving: A/B

Let _g_(_x_) be the transformation of _f_(_x_). Write the rule for _g_(_x_) using the change described.

1. reflection across the _y_-axis followed by a vertical shift 3 units up _____

2. horizontal stretch by a factor of 5 followed by a horizontal shift right 2 units _____

3. vertical compression by a factor of $\frac{1}{8}$ followed by a vertical shift down 6 units _____

4. reflection across the _x_-axis followed by a vertical stretch by a factor of 2, a horizontal shift 7 units left, and a vertical shift 5 units down _____

Use the graph to perform each transformation.

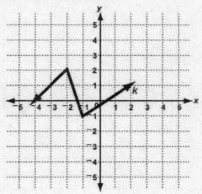

5. Transform _y_ = _k_(_x_) by compressing it horizontally by a factor of $\frac{1}{2}$.

   Label the new function _m_(_x_). Which coordinate is multiplied by $\frac{1}{2}$?

   _____

6. Transform _y_ = _k_(_x_) by translating it down 3 units. Label the new function _p_(_x_). What happens to the _y_-coordinate in each new ordered pair?

   _____

7. Transform _y_ = _k_(_x_) by stretching it vertically by a factor of 2. Label the new function _q_(_x_). Which coordinate is multiplied by 2?

   _____

8. Describe how the coordinates of a function change when the function is

   translated 2 units to the left and 4 units up. _____

LESSON 1-3
Transformations of Function Graphs
Practice and Problem Solving: C

Recall the graph of the ceiling function $f(x) = \lceil x \rceil$**, shown.**
The following situation describes a transformation of $f(x)$**:**

To rent a concert hall for one hour costs $40 plus an initial
cleaning fee of $120. There is a charge of $40 for every
additional hour or fraction of an hour thereafter.

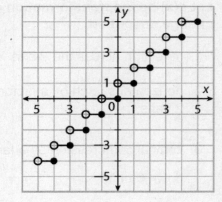

Use the description for Problems 1–6.

1. Write a transformation function $g(x)$ in terms of $f(x)$

   describing the cost of renting the concert hall.

   _____

2. Graph $g(x)$. Show the rental cost for up to 8 hours.

3. Describe the effect on the graph of $g(x)$ if the cleaning fee were
   changed to $80. Then write a transformation function $h(x)$ in terms of
   $g(x)$ based on this situation.

   _____

   _____

4. Graph $h(x)$. Show the rental cost for up to 8 hours.

5. Describe the effect on the graph of $g(x)$ if the rental fees were changed
   to $40 for every 2 hours. Then write a transformation function $j(x)$ in
   terms of $g(x)$ based on this situation.

   _____

   _____

6. Graph $j(x)$. Show the rental cost for up to 8 hours.

LESSON 1-4

Inverses of Functions

Practice and Problem Solving: A/B

Find the inverse of each function.

1. $f(x) = 10 - 4x$ _____

2. $g(x) = 15x - 10$ _____

3. $h(x) = \dfrac{x - 12}{4}$ _____

4. $j(x) = \dfrac{3x + 1}{6}$ _____

Find the inverse of each function. Then graph the function and its inverse.

5. $f(x) = 5x + 10$

6. $f(x) = \dfrac{9}{2}x - 5$

$f^{-1}(x) = $ _____

$f^{-1}(x) = $ _____

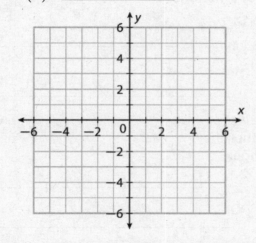

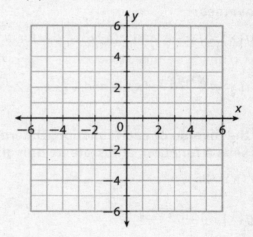

Use composition to determine whether each pair of functions are inverses.

7. $g(x) = -5 - \dfrac{7}{2}x$ and $f(x) = -\dfrac{2}{7}x - \dfrac{10}{7}$ _____

8. $s(x) = 7 - 2x$ and $t(x) = \dfrac{1}{2}x + \dfrac{7}{2}$ _____

9. $h(x) = \dfrac{1}{3}x + 4$ and $j(x) = 3x - 12$ _____

Name _____ Date _____ Class_____

LESSON 1-4 Inverses of Functions

Practice and Problem Solving: C

Determine whether the inverse of each relation is a function. If so, state whether the inverse is a one-to-one or a many-to-one function. If not, explain the reasoning.

1.

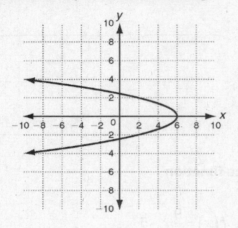

_____

2.

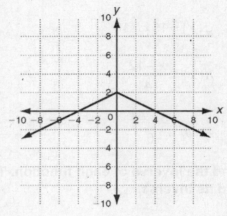

_____

Use composition to determine whether each pair of functions are inverses.

3. $g(x) = \sqrt{x} - 4$ and $r(x) = x^2 + 4$ for $x \geq 0$ _____

4. $u(x) = \dfrac{x^2}{4} - 1$ for $x \geq 1$ and $v(x) = \pm 2\sqrt{x+1}$ _____

Find the inverse of each function. Determine whether the inverse is a function, and state its domain and range.

5. $f(x) = 25 - x^2$ _____

6. $g(x) = 4 + \sqrt{2x - 1}$ _____

The area of a regular octagon can be found using the formula $A(s) = 2s^2(\sqrt{2} + 1)$, where s is the length of each side. Use this information for Problems 7–9.

7. Find the inverse, $A^{-1}(s)$. _____

8. What does the inverse represent? _____

9. What is the side length of a regular octagon whose area is $(9.68\sqrt{2} + 9.68)$ square meters? _____

LESSON 2-1 Graphing Absolute Value Functions
Practice and Problem Solving: A/B

Graph each function. Then identify the vertex, domain, and range.

1. $f(x) = |x| + 2$

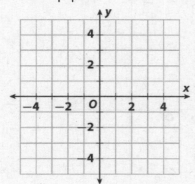

_____

2. $f(x) = -|x - 4|$

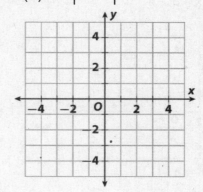

_____

3. $f(x) = -3|x| + 5$

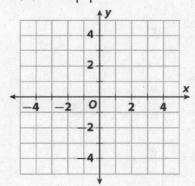

_____

4. $f(x) = |x + 1| - 1$

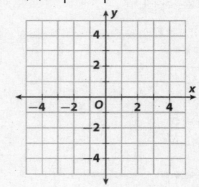

_____

Charles meets with customers on a daily basis. He uses the function
$f(x) = 5|x - 8| + 20$ **to calculate how many dollars he charges,**
per hour, for his time.

5. How much does Charles charge per hour if a customer hires him for 3 hours?

_____

6. Find the lowest hourly rate that Charles charges. Show your work.

_____

_____

Graphing Absolute Value Functions
Practice and Problem Solving: C

Graph each function. Then identify the vertex, domain, and range.

1. $f(x) = 2|x - 3| - 4$

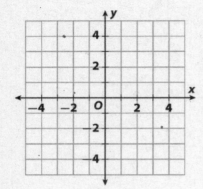

2. $f(x) = -\dfrac{1}{3}|-x + 2| + 2$

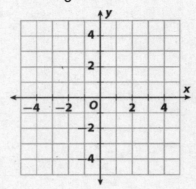

3. $f(x) = -|2x - 5| + 1$

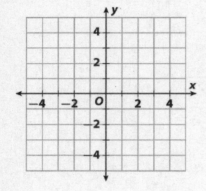

4. $f(x) = \dfrac{2}{3}|1 - x| - 2$

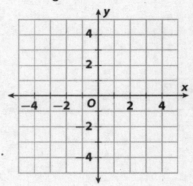

Solve.

5. Let a, b, and c be positive integers. Find the vertex, domain and range of the function $f(x) = |ax + b| + c$.

6. Rewrite the function $f(x) = |x + 1| - |x - 1|$ in piecewise form. State its domain and range.

LESSON 2-2 Solving Absolute Value Equations
Practice and Problem Solving: A/B

Solve.

1. How many solutions does the equation $|x + 7| = 1$ have?   _____

2. How many solutions does the equation $|x + 7| = 0$ have?   _____

3. How many solutions does the equation $|x + 7| = -1$ have?   _____

Solve each equation algebraically.

4. $|x| = 12$

5. $|x| = \dfrac{1}{2}$

6. $|x| - 6 = 4$

_____   _____   _____

7. $5 + |x| = 14$

8. $3|x| = 24$

9. $|x + 3| = 10$

_____   _____   _____

Solve each equation graphically.

10. $|x - 1| = 2$

11. $4|x - 5| = 12$

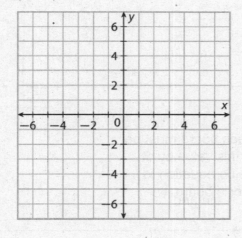   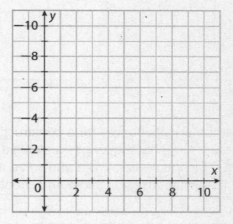

_____   _____

Leticia sets the thermostat in her apartment to 68 degrees. The actual temperature in her apartment can vary from this by as much as 3.5 degrees.

12. Write an absolute-value equation that you can

use to find the minimum and maximum temperature. _____

13. Solve the equation to find the minimum and

maximum temperature. _____

LESSON 2-2

Solving Absolute Value Equations

Practice and Problem Solving: C

Solve each equation algebraically.

1. $|x| + 6 = -4$

2. $-9|x| = -63$

3. $|x + 11| = 0$

_____   _____   _____

4. $\left|x - \dfrac{1}{2}\right| = 2$

5. $3|x - 1| = -15$

6. $|x - 1| - 1.4 = 6.2$

_____   _____   _____

Solve each equation graphically.

7. $\dfrac{|4x - 1|}{2} = 1$

8. $-3|5x - 2| = -12$

_____   _____

Solve.

9. A carpenter cuts boards for a construction project. Each board must be 3 meters long, but the length is allowed to differ from this value by at most 0.5 centimeters. Write and solve an absolute-value equation to find the minimum and maximum acceptable lengths for a board.

_____

_____

10. The owner of a butcher shop keeps the shop's freezer at −5°C. It is acceptable for the temperature to differ from this value by 1.5°. Write and solve an absolute-value equation to find the minimum and maximum acceptable temperatures.

_____

_____

LESSON 2-3

Solving Absolute Value Inequalities

Practice and Problem Solving: A/B

Solve each inequality and graph the solutions.

1. $|x| - 2 \leq 3$

_____

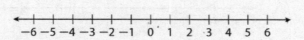

2. $|x + 1| + 5 < 7$

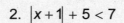
_____

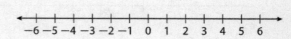

3. $3|x - 6| \leq 9$

_____

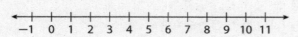

4. $|x + 3| - 1.5 < -2.5$

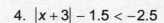
_____

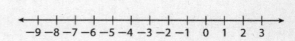

5. $|x| + 17 > 20$

_____

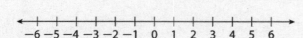

6. $|x - 6| - 7 > -3$

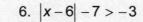
_____

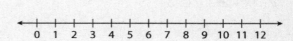

7. $\frac{1}{2}|x + 5| \geq 2$

_____

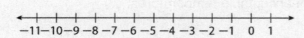

8. $2|x - 2| \geq 3$

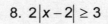
_____

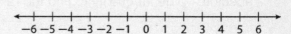

Solve.

9. The organizers of a drama club wanted to sell 350 tickets to their show. The actual sales were no more than 35 tickets from this goal. Write and solve an absolute-value inequality to find the range of the number of tickets that could have been sold.

_____

10. The temperature at noon in Los Angeles on a summer day was 88 °F. During the day, the temperature varied from this by as much as 7.5 °F. Write and solve an absolute-value inequality to find the range of possible temperatures for that day.

_____

Name _____ Date _____ Class_____

Solving Absolute Value Inequalities

Practice and Problem Solving: C

Solve each inequality and graph the solutions.

1. $|x| - 7 < -4$

_____

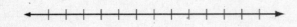

2. $|x - 3| + 0.7 < 2.7$

_____

3. $\frac{1}{3}|x + 2| \leq 1$

_____

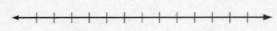

4. $|x - 5| - 3 > 1$

_____

5. $|5x| \geq 15$

_____

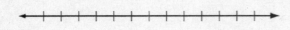

6. $\left|x + \frac{1}{2}\right| - 2 \geq 2$

_____

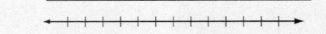

7. $|x - 2| + 7 \geq 3$

_____

8. $4|x - 6| \geq -8$

_____

Solve.

9. The ideal temperature for a refrigerator is 36.5 °F. It is acceptable for the temperature to differ from this value by at most 1.5 °F. Write and solve an absolute-value inequality to find the range of acceptable temperatures.

_____

10. At a trout farm, most of the trout have a length of 23.5 cm. The length of some of the trout differs from this by as much as 2.1 cm. Write and solve an absolute-value inequality to find the range of lengths of the trout.

_____

11. Ben says that there is no solution for this absolute-value inequality. Is he correct? If not, solve the inequality. Explain how you know you are correct.

$$32 + \frac{|x - 7|}{13} < 7$$

_____

_____

LESSON 3-1

Solving Quadratic Equations by Taking Square Roots
Practice and Problem Solving: A/B

For Problems 1–3, solve the equation $-2x^2 + 7 = -1$ using the indicated method. Show your work.

1. Solve by graphing.

2. Solve by factoring.

3. Solve by taking square roots.

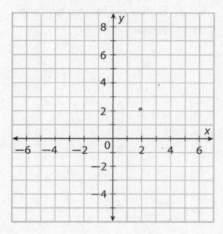

_____   _____   _____

Find the square of each imaginary number.

4. $4i$

5. $i\sqrt{11}$

6. $\dfrac{i\sqrt{7}}{3}$

_____   _____   _____

Determine whether each equation has real or imaginary solutions by solving.

7. $7x^2 - 12 = 0$

8. $x^2 + 9 = 3$

9. $2(x^2 - 1) = (x^2 - 3)$

_____   _____   _____

_____   _____   _____

Recall the equation for falling objects: $h(t) = h_0 - 16t^2$, where h is the height of the object, in feet, at any time t, in seconds, and h_0 is the object's initial height in feet. Use this equation for Problems 10–11.

10. A carpenter dropped a hammer from a rooftop 48 feet above ground. How long did it take the hammer to hit the ground?

_____

11. An acorn fell from a branch 20 feet high and landed on a branch 7 feet high. How long did it take the acorn to fall?

_____

LESSON 3-1

Solving Quadratic Equations by Taking Square Roots

Practice and Problem Solving: C

For Problems 1–3, solve the equation $\frac{1}{2}x^2 - 3 = 5$ using the indicated method. Show your work.

1. Solve by graphing.

2. Solve by factoring.

3. Solve by taking square roots.

_____ _____ _____

Find the square of each imaginary number.

4. $-21i$

5. $2i\sqrt{97}$

6. $-\dfrac{3i\sqrt{21}}{5}$

_____ _____ _____

Determine whether each equation has real or imaginary solutions by solving.

7. $\dfrac{1}{3}x^2 + 15 = -21$

8. $-15x^2 + 44 = 2$

9. $6\left(3x^2 - 1\right) = 3\left(5x^2 - 7\right)$

_____ _____ _____

_____ _____ _____

Solve.

10. The length of a rectangular garden is 4 times its width. The area is 102 square feet. What are the dimensions of the garden? _____

11. A rock fell from a cliff 108 feet high and landed on an embankment 25 feet from the ground. Use the equation $h = \dfrac{1}{2} \times 16 \times t^2$ to find how long it took the rock to fall to the embankment? _____

LESSON 3-2

Complex Numbers

Practice and Problem Solving: A/B

Write each expression as an imaginary number.

1. $\sqrt{-25}$

2. $3\sqrt{-49}$

3. $-\sqrt{-81}$

_____   _____   _____

For each complex number, identify the real part.

4. $2i$

5. $-3 + \sqrt{3} - 2i$

_____   _____

For each complex number, identify the imaginary part.

6. $\frac{1}{2}i - \frac{1}{3}$

7. $-\sqrt{5} + (1 - \sqrt{2})i$

_____   _____

Simplify each expression. Write your answer as a complex number.

8. $(4i) + (2 + 8i)$

9. $(2 - 7i) - (5 - 3i)$

10. $(3 + i)(1 - 4i)$

_____   _____   _____

11. In electronics, the total resistance to the flow of electricity in a circuit is called the *impedance*, Z. Impedance is represented by a complex number. The total impedance in a series circuit is the sum of individual impedances. The impedance in one part of a circuit is $Z_1 = 3 + 4i$. In another part of a circuit, the impedance is $Z_2 = 5 - 2i$. What is the total impedance of the circuit?

_____

12. In a circuit, the voltage V is given by the formula $V = IZ$, where I is the current and Z is the impedance. Both the current and the impedance are represented by complex numbers. Find the voltage if the current is $3 + 2i$ and the impedance is $4 - i$.

_____

LESSON 3-2

Complex Numbers

Practice and Problem Solving: C

Write each imaginary number as an expression without *i*.

1. $\sqrt{6}i - 9i^2$

2. $i^2 - i^4$

3. $2i + 5i^6$

_____   _____   _____

When simplified, what is the real part of the complex expression?

4. $(-1 + 2i) + (6 - 9i)$

5. $(3 - 3i) - (4 + 7i)$

_____   _____

When simplified, what is the imaginary part of the complex expression?

6. $(4 + 5i)(2 + i)$

7. $(3 + 2i)i^2$

_____   _____

Use the complex expression $\dfrac{-3 + 7i}{1 + 8i}$ to answer Problems 8 and 9.
(Recall that multiplication and division are inverse operations.)

8. Set up a multiplication problem that will help you simplify the complex expression so that the denominator is free of *i*.

9. What is the denominator of the expression when it is

   simplified? _____

10. a. Does $\sqrt{-3} \cdot \sqrt{-12} = \sqrt{(-3) \cdot (-12)}$? Explain.

   _____

   b. Write a general rule for the product of radicals when using complex numbers.

   _____

11. In a circuit, the voltage *V* is given by the formula $V = IZ$, where *I* is the current and *Z* is the impedance. Both the current and the impedance are represented by complex numbers. Find the voltage if the current is $2 - i^3$ and the impedance is $5 + 2i$.

   _____

LESSON 3-3

Finding Complex Solutions of Quadratic Equations
Practice and Problem Solving: A/B

Solve using the quadratic formula.

1. $x^2 + 10x = -9$

_____

2. $x^2 + 2x = -4$

_____

3. $x^2 + 5x = 3$

_____

4. $2x^2 + 7x + 10 = 0$

_____

Find the discriminant of each equation. Then determine the number of real or nonreal solutions.

5. $x^2 - 3x = -8$

_____

6. $x^2 + 4x = -3$

_____

7. $2x^2 - 12x = -18$

_____

Complete the square for each expression. Write the resulting expression as a binomial squared.

8. $x^2 - 4x + \boxed{}$

_____

9. $x^2 + 12x + \boxed{}$

_____

10. $25x^2 - 10x + \boxed{}$

_____

Solve each equation by completing the square.

11. $x^2 + 2x = 3$

_____

12. $2x^2 = 8 + 10x$

_____

13. $-3x^2 + 18x = -30$

_____

14. $4x^2 = -12x + 4$

_____

15. The height in meters of a baseball t seconds after it is hit straight up in the air with a velocity of 45 m/s is given by $h = -9.8t^2 + 45t + 1.2$. Will a baseball hit straight up with this velocity hit the roof of a batting cage with a maximum height of 64.5 m? Use the discriminant to explain your answer.

_____

_____

_____

_____

_____

Finding Complex Solutions of Quadratic Equations
Practice and Problem Solving: C

Solve using the quadratic formula.

1. $2x^2 - 6x - 1 = 0$

2. $x^2 - x = -12$

_____   _____

3. $-2x^2 = 5x - 20$

4. $-4x^2 - 3x - 36 = 0$

_____   _____

Find the discriminant of each equation. Then determine the number of real or nonreal solutions.

5. $2x^2 + 7 = -4x$

6. $x^2 - 3 = -6x$

7. $4x^2 + 4 = -8x$

_____   _____   _____

Complete the square for each expression. Write the resulting expression as a binomial squared.

8. $x^2 - 22x + \boxed{}$

9. $x^2 + 9x + \boxed{}$

10. $64x^2 - 48x + \boxed{}$

_____   _____   _____

Solve each equation by completing the square.

11. $14x + x^2 = 24$

12. $2x^2 - 8x = -2$

_____   _____

13. $x^2 = 3x + 4$

14. $4x^2 + 32x + 16 = 0$

_____   _____

15. A pedestrian suspension bridge built above a road is supported by a parabolic arch. The height in feet of the arch is given by the equation $h(x) = x(13.5 - x)$. Can a semi-truck with a height of 31.25 feet pass under the highest point of the arch? Use the discriminant to explain.

_____

_____

_____

_____

_____

Name _____ Date _____ Class _____

Circles

Practice and Problem Solving: A/B

Write the equation of each circle.

1. Center (8, 9) and radius $r = 10$

   _____

2. Center (–1, 5) and containing the point (23, –2)

   _____

3. Center (2, 2) and containing the point (–1, 6)

   _____

4. Center (3, –5) and containing the point (–7, 11)

   _____

5. Center (–3, 0) and radius $r = 6$

   _____

6. Center (6, –1) and radius $r = 8$

   _____

Graph each circle by rewriting the equations in standard form.

7. $x^2 + y^2 + 4x - 4y - 1 = 0$

   _____

8. $x^2 + y^2 + 2x + 4y + 1 = 0$

   _____

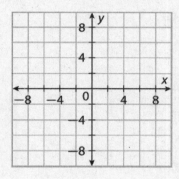

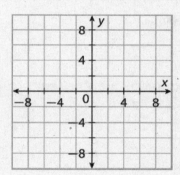

Solve.

9. A rock concert is located at the point (–1, 1). The music can be heard up to 4 miles away. Use the equation of a circle to find the locations that are affected. Assume each unit of the coordinate plane represents 1 mile.

   _____

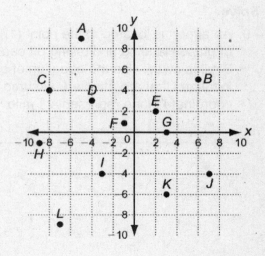

**LESSON
4-1**

Circles

Practice and Problem Solving: C

Write the equation of each circle.

1. Center $(9, -1)$ and radius $r = 7$

   _____

2. Center $(-5, -2)$ and containing the point $(19, -9)$

   _____

3. Center $(8, -3)$ and containing the point $(-2, 21)$

   _____

4. Center $(-5, 11)$ and containing the point $(-17, 2)$

   _____

5. Center $(0, -12)$ and radius $r = 10$

   _____

6. Center $(7, 8)$ and radius $r = 3$

   _____

Graph each circle by rewriting the equations in standard form.

7. $2x^2 + 2y^2 + 2x - 2y - 71 = 0$

   _____

8. $4x^2 + 4y^2 - 32x - 28y + 97 = 0$

   _____

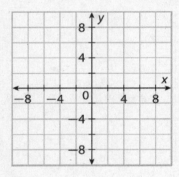
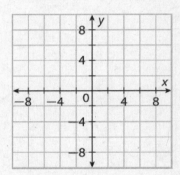

Solve.

9. An airport is located at the point $(1, -1)$. The noise of planes landing and taking off can be heard up to 3 miles away. Use the equation of a circle to find the locations that are affected. Assume each unit of the coordinate plane represents 1 mile.

   _____

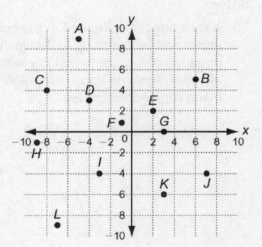

LESSON 4-2

Parabolas

Practice and Problem Solving: A/B

Use the Distance Formula to find the equation of a parabola with the given focus and directrix.

1. $F(6, 0)$, $x = -3$

2. $F(1, 0)$, $x = -4$

_____

_____

Write the equation in standard form for each parabola.

3. Vertex $(0, 0)$, directrix $y = -2$

4. Vertex $(0, 0)$, focus $(9, 0)$

_____

_____

5. Focus $(-6, 0)$, directrix $x = 6$

6. Vertex $(0, 0)$, focus $(0, -3)$

_____

_____

Find the vertex, value of p, axis of symmetry, focus, and directrix of each parabola. Then graph.

7. $x - 1 = -\dfrac{1}{12}y^2$

8. $y + 2 = \dfrac{1}{4}(x - 1)^2$

_____

_____

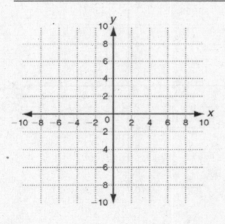

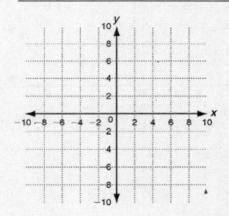

Solve.

9. A spotlight has parabolic cross sections.

   a. Write an equation for a cross section of the spotlight if the bulb is 6 inches from the vertex and the vertex is placed at the origin.

   _____

   b. If the spotlight has a diameter of 36 inches at its opening, find the depth of the spotlight if the bulb is 6 inches from the vertex.

   _____

| LESSON 4-2 | **Parabolas** |

Practice and Problem Solving: C

Write the equation in standard form for each parabola.

1. Vertex (0, 0), directrix $y = 6$

_____

2. Vertex (0, 0), focus (5, 0)

_____

3. Vertex (0, 0), focus (10, 0)

_____

4. Vertex (0, 0), directrix $y = -4$

_____

5. Focus (−1, 0), directrix $x = 3$

_____

6. Vertex (4, 6), focus (4, −2)

_____

Find the vertex, value of p, axis of symmetry, focus, and directrix of each parabola. Then graph.

7. $x - 2 = \dfrac{1}{2}(y + 3)^2$

_____

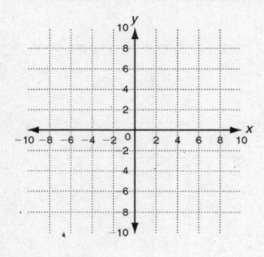

8. $y + 1 = -(x - 2)^2$

_____

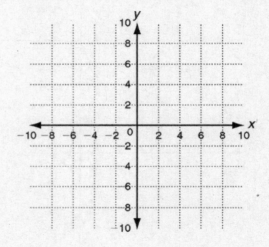

Solve.

9. A spotlight has parabolic cross sections.

a. Write an equation for a cross section of the spotlight if the bulb is 15 centimeters from the vertex and the vertex is placed at the origin.

_____

b. If the spotlight has a diameter of 72 centimeters at its opening, find the depth of the spotlight if the bulb is 15 centimeters from the vertex.

_____

LESSON 4-3
Solving Linear-Quadratic Systems
Practice and Problem Solving: A/B

Solve each system represented by the functions graphically.

1. $\begin{cases} y - x^2 = -4 \\ y - 2x = -1 \end{cases}$

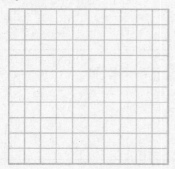

_____

2. $\begin{cases} y - x^2 + 4x - 6 = 0 \\ y + x = 4 \end{cases}$

_____

Solve each system algebraically.

3. $\begin{cases} 9y - 6x = 0 \\ \dfrac{x^2}{45} + \dfrac{y^2}{5} = 1 \end{cases}$

_____

4. $\begin{cases} x^2 + y^2 = 101 \\ 10x + y = 0 \end{cases}$

_____

5. $\begin{cases} 3y = 4x \\ x^2 - y^2 = -63 \end{cases}$

_____

6. $\begin{cases} 8y = x + 5 \\ x + 5 = \dfrac{1}{2}y^2 \end{cases}$

_____

7. $\begin{cases} x^2 + y^2 = 34 \\ 3x - 3y = 6 \end{cases}$

_____

8. $\begin{cases} -x^2 + 12x + 4y - 84 = 0 \\ 2x + y = 1 \end{cases}$

_____

Solve.

9. A model airplane takes off at a constant rate of 15 feet per second. Its height, in feet, after t seconds is given by $h = 15t$. At the same time, a ball is launched from ground level with an initial velocity of 45 feet per second. The height of the ball, in feet, after t seconds is given by $h = -16t^2 + 45t$. Will the airplane and ball collide? If so, find the time it takes for the collision to occur.

_____

LESSON 4-3

Solving Linear-Quadratic Systems

Practice and Problem Solving: C

Solve each system. If necessary, use the Quadratic Formula.

1. $\begin{cases} y = -4x \\ x + 1 = \dfrac{1}{8}y^2 \end{cases}$

2. $\begin{cases} -x^2 + 4x + 15y - 92 = 0 \\ x - 2y = 3 \end{cases}$

_____

3. $\begin{cases} \dfrac{y^2}{9} - \dfrac{x^2}{9} = 1 \\ 4y = 5x \end{cases}$

4. $\begin{cases} 21x - 14y = 0 \\ \dfrac{3x^2}{16} + \dfrac{y^2}{6} = 1 \end{cases}$

_____

5. $\begin{cases} x - 2y = -1 \\ -6x^2 + 2y^2 + 3x + 11y = 62 \end{cases}$

6. $\begin{cases} x + y + 3 = 0 \\ -4x^2 + 5y^2 - 24x + 2y - 71 = 0 \end{cases}$

_____

Jordon and Katherine are jogging on paths in a state park. Jordon's jogging path can be modeled by the equation $x + y = 25$. Katherine's jogging path can be modeled by the equation $\dfrac{y^2}{60^2} + \dfrac{x^2}{40^2} = 1$.

Meanwhile, a ranger is driving through the park on a road modeled by the equation $y - 5(x - 30) = -70$. Use this information for Problems 7–9.

7. Will Jordon's and Katherine's paths intersect? If so, at what points? If not, explain your reasoning.

_____

_____

8. Will the ranger cross paths with Katherine? If so, at what points? If not, explain your reasoning.

_____

_____

9. Will the ranger cross paths with Jordon? If so, at what points? If not, explain your reasoning.

_____

_____

LESSON 4-4

Solving Linear Systems in Three Variables

Practice and Problem Solving: A/B

Solve each system using substitution.

1. $\begin{cases} x + y + 2z = -7 \\ -5z = 25 \\ 3x - 3y - 6z = 3 \end{cases}$

2. $\begin{cases} 20x + 20y = 46 \\ 50x + 20z = 126 \\ 60x + 10y + 50z = 263 \end{cases}$

_____   _____

Solve each system using elimination.

3. $\begin{cases} -r + 6s - 4t = 17 \\ -4r - s - 4t = 7 \\ -r + s + 5t = -15 \end{cases}$

4. $\begin{cases} 3r + 2s + 3t = -2 \\ -3r + s - 2t = -1 \\ 6r + s + 5t = -1 \end{cases}$

_____   _____

Solve each system using matrices.

5. $\begin{cases} -3b + c = 15 \\ -2a + 3b + 2c = 11 \\ -3a - 4b + c = 30 \end{cases}$

6. $\begin{cases} x + y + 2z = 9 \\ 3x - 4y = 16 \\ -3x - 3y - 6z = 0 \end{cases}$

_____   _____

Solve.

7. Steve is cashing in his jar of spare nickels, dimes, and quarters. When he gets to the bank, he receives a total of $14.70. He learns that he had 133 coins in all, and that there were 3 times as many dimes as quarters. How many of each type of coin did he save?

   a. Write a system of equations that models this situation.

   _____

   b. Solve the system using any method. How many of each type of coin did Steve save?

   _____

Solving Linear Systems in Three Variables

LESSON 4-4

Practice and Problem Solving: C

Solve each system using substitution.

1. $\begin{cases} \dfrac{1}{2}x + z = -4 \\ y - \dfrac{1}{3}z = 5 \\ x - \dfrac{3}{2}y = -8 \end{cases}$ $x =$ $y =$ $z =$

(____ , ____ , ____)

2. $\begin{cases} 0.5x - 2.5y + 3z = -4.05 \\ 2.5y + 2z = -4.35 \\ 1.2y - 0.8z = 1.08 \end{cases}$

_____

Solve each system using elimination.

3. $\begin{cases} -30x - 50y - 40z = -61 \\ -50x - 60y - 50z = -142 \\ -6x - y = -21 \end{cases}$

(____ , ____ , ____)

4. $\begin{cases} -x - 2y - 2z = -\dfrac{23}{6} \\ -\dfrac{5}{3}x + \dfrac{2}{3}y - 2z = \dfrac{29}{18} \\ -x + y - z = \dfrac{13}{6} \end{cases}$

_____

Solve each system using matrices.

5. $\begin{cases} 0.4a - 0.8b - 0.8c = 0.8 \\ 2a + 2b - 1.2c = 4.8 \\ 0.2a + 0.6b = 0.8 \end{cases}$

_____

6. $\begin{cases} 3r + 2s + t = -2 \\ 15r + 6s - 9t = -4 \\ -12r - 15t = -4 \end{cases}$

_____

Solve each system using any method.

7. $\begin{cases} 50x - 50y = -45 \\ -60x + 60y = -66 \\ 4y - 2z = -14 \end{cases}$

_____

8. $\begin{cases} 30x + 20y + 30z = 118 \\ 10x + 10y - 20z = -119 \\ 10x + 40y + 40z = 172 \end{cases}$

_____

Solve.

9. At the beginning of the year, Francesca opened 3 investment accounts with a total of $5450. Over the year, Account A earned 6% interest, Account B earned 5% interest, and account C earned 4% interest. By year's end, she had earned a total of $286.50 in interest. How much were the original deposits in each account if she deposited twice as much in Account A as she did in Account C?

_____

LESSON 5-1 Graphing Cubic Functions

Practice and Problem Solving: A/B

Calculate the reference points for each transformation of the parent function $f(x) = x^3$. Then graph the transformation. (The graph of the parent function is shown.)

1. $g(x) = (x - 3)^3 + 2$

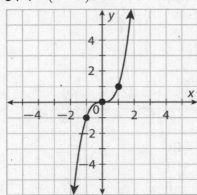

_____

2. $g(x) = -3(x + 2)^3 - 2$

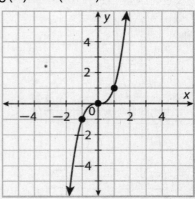

_____

Write the equation of the cubic function whose graph is shown.

3.

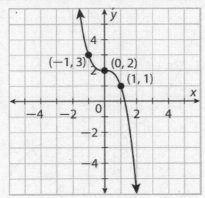

4.

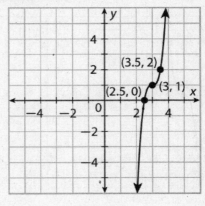

_____

_____

Solve.

5. The graph of $f(x) = x^3$ is reflected across the *x*-axis. The graph is then translated 11 units up and 7 units to the left. Write the equation of the transformed function.

_____

_____

6. The graph of $f(x) = x^3$ is stretched vertically by a factor of 6. The graph is then translated 9 units to the right and 3 units down. Write the equation of the transformed function.

_____

LESSON 5-1

Graphing Cubic Functions

Practice and Problem Solving: C

Calculate the reference points for each transformation of the parent function $f(x) = x^3$. Then graph the transformation. (The graph of the parent function is shown.)

1. $g(x) = -\dfrac{5}{2}(x-3)^3 + \dfrac{1}{2}$

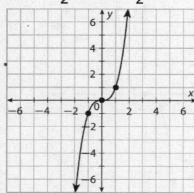

2. $g(x) = 1.25(x+5)^3 - 1.25$

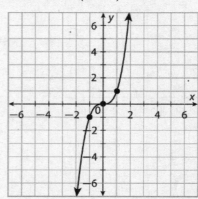

Write the equation of the cubic function whose graph is shown.

3.

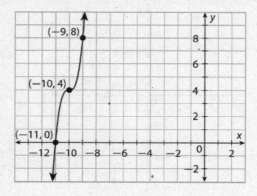

4.

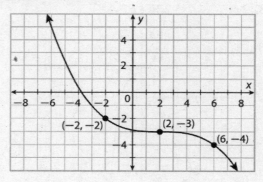

Solve.

5. The graph of the function $y = 3(x-2)^3 + 7$ is translated 2 units to the right and then 4 units down. Write the equation of the final graph.

_____

6. The graph of the function $y = (x)^3 + 5$ is translated 2 units to the left and then reflected across the *x*-axis. Write the equation of the final graph.

_____

LESSON 5-2

Graphing Polynomial Functions

Practice and Problem Solving: A/B

Identify whether the function graphed has an odd or even degree and a positive or negative leading coefficient.

1.

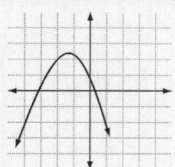

_____

2.

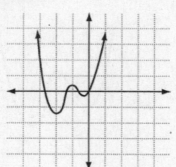

_____

3.

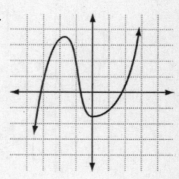

_____

Use a graphing calculator to determine the number of turning points and the number and type (global or local) of any maximum or minimum values.

4. $f(x) = x(x-4)^2$

_____

5. $f(x) = -x^2(x-2)(x+1)$

_____

Graph the function. State the end behavior, *x*-intercepts, and intervals where the function is above or below the *x*-axis.

6. $f(x) = -(x-1)^2(x+3)$

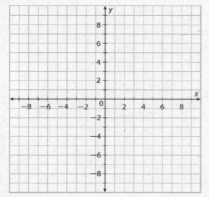

7. $f(x) = (x+2)(x-3)(x-1)$

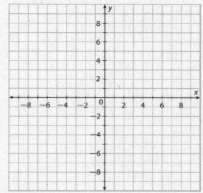

End behavior: _____

x-intercepts: _____

Above *x*-axis: _____

Below *x* axis: _____

End behavior: _____

x-intercepts: _____

Above *x*-axis: _____

Below *x*-axis: _____

**LESSON
5-2**

Graphing Polynomial Functions

Practice and Problem Solving: C

**Identify whether the function graphed has an odd or even degree and
a positive or negative leading coefficient.**

1.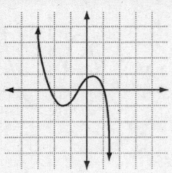
_____

2.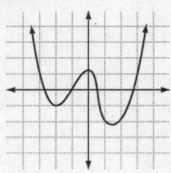
_____

3.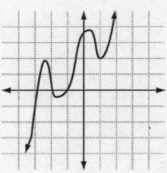
_____

**Use a graphing calculator to determine the number of turning points
and the number and type (global or local) of any maximum or
minimum values.**

4. $f(x) = -(x-1)^3(x+2)$

5. $f(x) = x^5(x-3)(x+2)$

_____

**Graph the function. State the end behavior, x-intercepts, and intervals
where the function is above or below the x-axis.**

6. $f(x) = (x-2)^2(x+2)(x+3)$

7. $f(x) = -(x-1)^3(x+2)^2(x-3)$

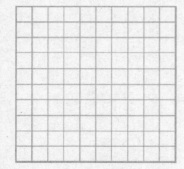

End behavior: _____

x-intercepts: _____

Above x-axis: _____

Below x axis: _____

End behavior: _____

x-intercepts: _____

Above x-axis: _____

Below x-axis: _____

LESSON
6-1

Adding and Subtracting Polynomials

Practice and Problem Solving: A/B

Identify the degree of each monomial.

1. $6x^2$

2. $3p^3m^4$

3. $2x^8y^3$

_____

_____

_____

Rewrite each polynomial in standard form. Then identify the leading coefficient, degree, and number of terms.

4. $6 + 7x - 4x^3 + x^2$

_____

5. $x^2 - 3 + 2x^5 + 7x^4 - 12x$

_____

Add or subtract. Write your answer in standard form.

6. $(2x^2 - 2x + 6) + (11x^3 - x^2 - 2 + 5x)$

7. $(x^2 - 8) - (3x^3 - 6x - 4 + 9x^2)$

_____

_____

8. $(5x^4 + x^2) + (7 + 9x^2 - 2x^4 + x^3)$

9. $(12x^2 + x) - (6 - 9x^2 + x^7 - 8x)$

_____

_____

Solve.

10. An accountant finds that the gross income, in thousands of dollars, of a small business can be modeled by the polynomial $-0.3t^2 + 8t + 198$, where t is the number of years after 2010. The yearly expenses of the business, in thousands of dollars, can be modeled by the polynomial $-0.2t^2 + 2t + 131$.

   a. Find a polynomial that predicts the net profit of the business after t years.

   _____

   b. Assuming that the models continue to hold, how much net profit can the business expect to make in the year 2016?

   _____

LESSON 6-1 Adding and Subtracting Polynomials

Practice and Problem Solving: C

Rewrite each polynomial in standard form. Then identify the leading coefficient, degree, and number of terms.

1. $5x^3 + 2x - 1 - 10x^2 + 9x^5 - 3x^4$

_____

Add or subtract. Write your answer in standard form.

2. $(7x^3 + 2x - 1) + (8x^2 - 6 + 2x - x^3)$

_____

3. $(12 - 11x - 5x^5) - (4x^4 + 8x - 4x^5 + 2x^3 - 1)$

_____

4. $(-3x^4 + x^6 - 9x^5 + 2x^2 - 7) - (-2x^5 + x - 4x^2 - x^4 + 12)$

_____

Solve.

5. What polynomial could you add to $3x^4 - 9x^3 + 5x^2 - x + 7$ to get a sum of $3 + 4x^4 + 3x - x^3 + 3x^2$?

_____

6. What polynomial could you subtract from $5x^3 - 12x - x^2 + 9 - 12x^5 - 6x^4$ to give a difference of $19 + 8x^3 - 18x - 19x^5 - 2x^2 - 8x^4$?

_____

7. The profit earned by the sales division of a company each year can be modeled by the polynomial $x^3 - x^2 + 2x - 100$, where x is the number of units sold. The profit earned by the manufacturing division can be modeled with the polynomial $x^2 - 4x - 300$.

   a. Write a polynomial to represent the difference of the profit from the sales division and the profit from the manufacturing division.

   _____

   b. What is the total amount of profit that the company earns from both divisions?

   _____

**LESSON
6-2**

Multiplying Polynomials

Practice and Problem Solving: A/B

Find each product.

1. $4x^2(3x^2 + 1)$

_____

2. $-9x(x^2 + 2x + 4)$

_____

3. $-6x^2(x^3 + 7x^2 - 4x + 3)$

_____

4. $x^3(-4x^3 + 10x^2 - 7x + 2)$

_____

5. $-5m^3(7n^4 - 2mn^3 + 6)$

_____

6. $(x + 2)(y^2 + 2y - 12)$

_____

7. $(p + q)(4p^2 - p - 8q^2 - q)$

_____

8. $(2x^2 + xy - y)(y^2 + 3x)$

_____

Expand each expression.

9. $(3x - 1)^3$

_____

10. $(x - 4)^4$

_____

11. $3(a - 4b)^2$

_____

12. $5(x^2 - 2y)^3$

_____

Solve.

13. A biologist has found that the number of branches on a certain rare tree in its first few years of life can be modeled by the polynomial $b(y) = 4y^2 + y$. The number of leaves on each branch can be modeled by the polynomial $l(y) = 2y^3 + 3y^2 + y$, where y is the number of years after the tree reaches a height of 6 feet. Write a polynomial describing the total number of leaves on the tree.

_____

LESSON 6-2

Multiplying Polynomials

Practice and Problem Solving: C

Consider the expansion of $(x + y)^n$.

1. How many terms does the expression contain? _____

2. What is the exponent of x in the first term? _____

3. What is the exponent of y in the first term? _____

4. What is the sum of the exponents in any term of the expansion? _____

Find each product.

5. $-y^3(10x^2 + 4xy - y^2)$

_____

6. $(2a - b)^3$

_____

7. $5(h - 2)^4$

_____

8. $(2m^2 + n)(3n^2 + 6mn - m^2)$

_____

9. $\left(\dfrac{1}{3}x + 4\right)^3$

_____

10. $(4x - 5)(2x^5 + x^3 - 1)$

_____

11. $(a^3 + a^2b^2)(b^4 + a^2)$

_____

12. $(k^4 + k^3 + 12)(k^2 - k - 9)$

_____

Solve.

13. The momentum of an object is defined as its mass m multiplied by its velocity. As a certain experimental aircraft burns fuel, its mass decreases according to the polynomial $m(t) = 3000 - 0.1t^2 - 4t$, where m is in kilograms and t is measured in minutes since takeoff. Under the force of the engines, the velocity of the aircraft increases according to the function $v(t) = 0.001t^3 + 0.01t$, where v is in kilometers per second. What is the momentum of the rocket?

_____

LESSON
6-3

The Binomial Theorem

Practice and Problem Solving: A/B

Use the Binomial Theorem to expand each binomial.

1. $(x + y)^3$

_____

2. $(2x + y)^4$

_____

3. $(m + 3n)^3$

_____

4. $(p + q)^5$

_____

Solve.

5. Of the new cars in a car dealer's lot, 1 in 6 are white. Today, 4 cars were sold.

   a. What is the probability that 3 of the cars sold were white?

   _____

   b. What is the probability that at least 2 of the cars sold were white?

   _____

6. At a small college, $\frac{1}{3}$ of all of the students are vegetarians. There are
   5 students in line at the cafeteria.

   a. What is the probability that all 5 students are vegetarians?

   _____

   b. What is the probability that just 1 of the students is a vegetarian?

   _____

7. Ellen plays 8 hands of a card game with her friends. She has a 1 in 3
   chance of winning each hand. What is the probability that she will win
   exactly half of the hands played?

   _____

8. In a lottery, each ticket buyer has a 1 in 10 chance of winning a prize.
   If Chip buys 10 tickets, what is the probability that he will win at least
   1 prize?

   _____

The Binomial Theorem

LESSON 6-3

Practice and Problem Solving: C

Use the Binomial Theorem to expand each binomial.

1. $(x + y)^5$

   _____

2. $(4x + y)^4$

   _____

3. $(2x + y)^5$

   _____

4. $(n + 2m)^4$

   _____

Solve.

5. At Hopewell High School, 1 in 7 students is on a sports team. There are 4 student council representatives in the school.

   a. What is the probability that 2 of the student council representatives are also on a sports team?

   _____

   b. What is the probability that at least 3 of the student council representatives are on a sports team?

   _____

6. A donut shop sells donuts with a jelly filling. Two in every 5 donuts have a jelly filling. There are 5 donuts left in the package.

   a. What is the probability that all 5 donuts have a jelly filling?

   _____

   b. What is the probability that none of the donuts has a jelly filling?

   _____

7. Andrew is choosing CDs from a bag of free CDs without looking. He has a 1 in 5 chance of choosing a CD that he likes. He chooses 8 CDs in all. What is the probability that he will get 3 CDs that he likes?

   _____

8. In a game of bingo, the contestants have a 1 in 12 chance of winning each round. If Shirley plays 6 rounds, what is the probability that she will win at least half of them?

   _____

LESSON 6-4 Factoring Polynomials
Practice and Problem Solving: A/B

Simplify each polynomial, if possible. Then factor it.

1. $3n^2 - 48$

_____

2. $3x^3 - 75x$

_____

3. $9m^4 - 16$

_____

4. $16r^4 - 9$

_____

5. $3n^6 - 12$

_____

6. $x^6 - 9$

_____

7. $3b^7 + 12b^4 + 12b$

_____

8. $50v^6 + 60v^3 + 18$

_____

9. $x^3 - 64$

_____

10. $x^3 - 125$

_____

11. $x^6 - 64$

_____

12. $x^6 - 1$

_____

Factor each polynomial by grouping.

13. $8n^3 - 7n^2 + 56n - 49$

_____

14. $5x^3 - 6x^2 - 15x + 18$

_____

15. $9r^3 + 3r^2 - 21r - 7$

_____

16. $25v^3 + 25v^2 - 15v - 15$

_____

17. $120b^3 + 105b^2 + 200b + 175$

_____

18. $120x^3 - 80x^2 - 168x + 112$

_____

Solve.

19. A square concert stage in the center of a fairground has an area of $4x^2 + 12x + 9$ ft^2. The dimensions of the stage have the form $cx + d$, where c and d are whole numbers. Find an expression for the perimeter of the stage. What is the perimeter when $x = 2$ ft?

_____

LESSON
6-4

Factoring Polynomials

Practice and Problem Solving: C

Simplify each polynomial. Then factor it.

1. $12v^4 - 75$

_____

2. $5p^6 - 80$

_____

3. $20u^6 - 20u^3v^3 + 5v^6$

_____

4. $4x^6 - 32x^3y^3 + 64y^6$

_____

5. $8x^3 + 125$

_____

6. $64x^6 - 1$

_____

Factor each polynomial by grouping. Be sure to factor the polynomial completely.

7. $b^3 - 2b^2 - b + 2$

_____

8. $24v^3 + 56v^2 - 15v - 35$

_____

9. $245n^3 - 175n^2 - 196n + 140$

_____

10. $140x^6 + 100x^5 - 28x^4 - 20x^3$

_____

11. $150u^2v + 75u - 125u^2 - 90uv$

_____

12. $196x^2y - 64x + 56x^2 - 224xy$

_____

Solve.

13. Fatima has an herb garden. She grows parsley in a triangular section having an area of $\frac{1}{2}(3x^2 - 6x - x + 2)$ ft². What are the dimensions for the base and height of the parsley section?

_____

14. The voltage generated by an electrical circuit changes over time according to the polynomial $V(t) = t^3 - 4t^2 - 25t + 100$, where V is in volts and t is in seconds. Factor the polynomial to find the times when the voltage is equal to zero.

_____

LESSON 6-5 Dividing Polynomials
Practice and Problem Solving: A/B

Divide by using long division.

1. $(x^2 - x - 6) \div (x - 3)$

2. $(2x^3 - 10x^2 + x - 5) \div (x - 5)$

_____

_____

3. $(-3x^2 + 20x - 12) \div (x - 6)$

4. $(3x^3 + 9x^2 - 14) \div (x + 3)$

_____

_____

Divide by using synthetic division.

5. $(3x^2 - 8x + 4) \div (x - 2)$

6. $(5x^2 - 4x + 12) \div (x + 3)$

_____

_____

7. $(9x^2 - 7x + 3) \div (x - 1)$

8. $(-6x^2 + 5x - 10) \div (x + 7)$

_____

_____

Use synthetic substitution to evaluate $P(x)$ for the given value.

9. $P(x) = 4x^2 - 9x + 2$ for $x = 3$

10. $P(x) = -3x^2 + 10x - 4$ for $x = -2$

_____

_____

Determine whether the given binomial is a factor of $P(x)$.

11. $(x - 4)$; $P(x) = x^2 + 8x - 48$

12. $(x + 5)$; $P(x) = 2x^2 - 6x - 1$

_____

_____

Solve.

13. The total number of dollars donated each year to a small charitable organization
    has followed the trend $d(t) = 2t^3 + 10t^2 + 2000t + 10,000$, where d is dollars and t
    is the number of years since 1990. The total number of donors each year has
    followed the trend $p(t) = t^2 + 1000$. Write an expression describing the average
    number of dollars per donor.

_____

LESSON 6-5

Dividing Polynomials

Practice and Problem Solving: C

Divide by using long division.

1. $(2x^3 + 14x^2 - 4x - 48) \div (2x + 4)$

2. $(x^3 + 12x^2 - 4) \div (x - 3)$

_____

3. $(12x^4 + 23x^3 - 9x^2 + 15x + 4) \div (3x - 1)$

4. $(-2x^3 + 11x^2 - 8x - 7) \div (2x + 1)$

_____

Divide by using synthetic division.

5. $(9x^2 - 3x + 11) \div (x - 6)$

6. $(3x^4 - 2x^2 + 1) \div (x + 2)$

_____

7. $(6x^5 - 3x^2 + x - 2) \div (x - 1)$

8. $(-x^4 - 7x^3 + 6x^2 - 1) \div (x - 3)$

_____

Use synthetic substitution to evaluate $P(x)$ for the given value.

9. $P(x) = 4x^3 - 12x - 2$ for $x = 5$

10. $P(x) = -3x^4 + 5x^3 - x + 7$ for $x = -2$

_____

Use the Factor Theorem to verify that the given binomial is a factor of $P(x)$. Then divide.

11. $(x + 5); P(x) = 2x^2 + 6x - 20$

12. $(x - 1); P(x) = x^4 - 6x^3 + 4x^2 + 1$

_____

Solve.

13. The total weight of the cargo entering a seaport each year can be modeled by the function $C(t) = 0.2t^3 + 1000t^2 + 10t + 50,000$, where t is the number of years since the port was opened. The average weight of cargo delivered by each ship is modeled by the function $A(t) = 0.1t + 500$. Write an expression describing the number of ships entering the port each year.

_____

LESSON 7-1 Finding Rational Solutions of Polynomial Equations

Practice and Problem Solving: A/B

Solve each polynomial equation by factoring.

1. $4x^3 + x^2 - 4x - 1 = 0$

   _____

2. $x^5 - 2x^4 - 24x^3 = 0$

   _____

3. $3x^5 + 18x^4 - 21x^3 = 0$

   _____

4. $-x^4 + 2x^3 + 8x^2 = 0$

   _____

Identify the rational zeros of each function. Then write the function in factored form.

5. $f(x) = x^3 + 3x^2 + 3x + 1$

   _____

6. $f(x) = x^3 + 5x^2 - 8x - 48$

   _____

Identify all the rational roots of each equation.

7. $x^3 + 10x^2 + 17x = 28$

   _____

8. $3x^3 + 10x^2 - 27x = 10$

   _____

Solve.

9. An engineer is designing a storage compartment in a spacecraft. The compartment must be 2 meters longer than it is wide, and its depth must be 1 meter less than its width. The volume of the compartment must be 8 cubic meters.

   a. Write an equation to model the volume of the compartment.

   _____

   b. List all possible rational roots. _____

   c. Use synthetic division to find the roots of the polynomial equation. Are the roots all rational numbers?

   _____

   d. What are the dimensions of the storage compartment? _____

LESSON 7-1

Finding Rational Solutions of Polynomial Equations

Practice and Problem Solving: C

Solve each polynomial equation by factoring.

1. $-3x^4 + 6x^3 + 105x^2 = 0$

2. $8x^7 - 56x^6 + 96x^5 = 0$

_____ _____

Identify the rational zeros of each function. Then write the function in factored form.

3. $f(x) = x^3 + 6x^2 + 12x - 8$

4. $f(x) = x^3 + 10x^2 + 32x + 32$

_____ _____

Identify all the rational roots of each equation.

5. $x^3 + 2x^2 - 48x = 0$

6. $5x^4 + 19x^3 - 29x^2 + 5x = 0$

_____ _____

7. $6x^3 + 12x^2 - 18x = 0$

8. $3x^4 + 5x^3 - 11x^2 + 3x = 0$

_____ _____

Solve.

9. A jewelry box is designed such that its length is twice its width and its depth is 2 inches less than its width. The volume of the box is 64 cubic inches.

    a. Write an equation to model the volume of the box.

    _____

    b. List all possible rational roots. _____

    c. Use synthetic division to find the roots of the polynomial equation. Are the roots all rational numbers?

    _____

    d. What are the dimensions of the box? _____

LESSON 7-2

Finding Complex Solutions of Polynomial Equations

Practice and Problem Solving: A/B

Write the simplest polynomial function with the given roots.

1. 1, 4, and −3

2. $\frac{1}{2}$, 5, and −2

_____

_____

3. $2i$, $\sqrt{3}$, and 4

4. $\sqrt{2}$, −5, and −$3i$

_____

_____

Solve each equation by finding all roots.

5. $x^4 - 2x^3 - 14x^2 - 2x - 15 = 0$

6. $x^4 - 16 = 0$

_____

_____

7. $x^4 + 4x^3 + 4x^2 + 64x - 192 = 0$

8. $x^3 + 3x^2 + 9x + 27 = 0$

_____

_____

Solve.

9. An electrical circuit is designed such that its output voltage, *V*, measured in volts, can be either positive or negative. The voltage of the circuit passes through zero at *t* = 1, 2, and 7 seconds. Write the simplest polynomial describing the voltage *V*(*t*).

_____

LESSON 7-2

Finding Complex Solutions of Polynomial Equations

Practice and Problem Solving: C

Write the simplest polynomial function with the given roots.

1. $-\dfrac{3}{4}, 6$, and -1

2. $-5i, 2$, and 7

_____

3. $-i, -3$, and -1

4. $2i, 4$, and $\sqrt{6}$

_____

Solve each equation by finding all roots.

5. $4x^4 - 8x^3 - 3x^2 - 18x - 27 = 0$

6. $x^4 + 3x^3 - x^2 + 9x - 12 = 0$

_____

7. $x^4 - 3x^3 - 8x^2 + 22x - 24 = 0$

8. $x^3 + 6x^2 + 4x + 24 = 0$

_____

Solve.

9. For a scientific experiment, Tony needs a glass bell jar in the shape of a cylinder with a hemisphere on top. The height of the cylinder must be 3 inches longer than its radius, and the volume must be 72π cubic inches. What should the radius of the cylinder be?

_____

LESSON 8-1

Graphing Simple Rational Functions

Practice and Problem Solving: A/B

Using the graph of $f(x) = \dfrac{1}{x}$ as a guide, describe
the transformation and graph the function.

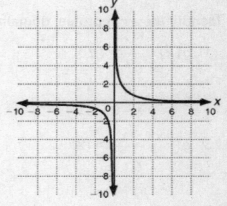

1. $g(x) = \dfrac{2}{x+4}$

    _____

Identify the asymptotes, domain, and range of each function.

2. $g(x) = \dfrac{1}{x-3} + 5$ _____

    _____

3. $g(x) = \dfrac{1}{x+8} - 1$ _____

    _____

Identify the asymptotes of the function. Then graph.

4. $f(x) = \dfrac{x^2 + 4x - 5}{x+1}$

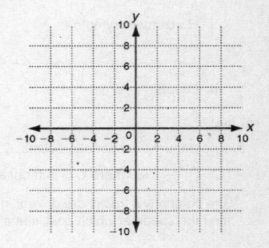

    a. Vertical asymptote:

    _____

    b. Horizontal asymptote:

    _____

    c. Graph.

Solve.

5. The number n of daily visitors to a new store can be modeled by the function
   $n = \dfrac{(250x + 1000)}{x}$, where x is the number of days the store has been open.

    a. What is the horizontal asymptote of this function
       and what does it represent?   _____

    b. To the nearest integer, how many
       visitors can be expected on day 30?   _____

LESSON 8-1

Graphing Simple Rational Functions

Practice and Problem Solving: C

Identify the asymptotes, domain, and range of each function.

1. $g(x) = \dfrac{1}{x+5} + 7$ _____

2. $g(x) = \dfrac{4}{x-9} - \dfrac{1}{4}$ _____

3. $g(x) = \dfrac{1}{x+\dfrac{2}{3}} - 12$ _____

Identify the zeros and asymptotes of the function. Then graph.

4. $f(x) = \dfrac{x^2 - 4x + 3}{4x + 4}$

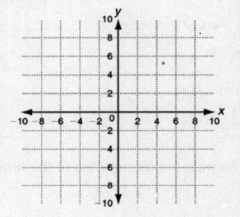

   a. Zeros:

   _____

   b. Vertical asymptote:

   _____

   c. Horizontal asymptote:

   _____

   d. Graph.

Solve.

5. The annual transportation costs, C, incurred by a company follow the formula

   $C = \dfrac{2500}{s} + s$, where C is in thousands of dollars and s is the average speed

   the company's trucks are driven, in miles per hour. Use your graphing calculator to
   find the speed at which cost is at a minimum.

   _____

LESSON 8-2

Graphing More Complicated Rational Functions

Practice and Problem Solving: A/B

Identify all vertical asymptotes and holes of each rational function. Then state its domain.

1. $f(x) = \dfrac{x-1}{-3x^2+27}$

   Vertical Asymptotes: _____

   Holes: _____

   Domain: _____

2. $f(x) = \dfrac{-x^2-3x+4}{x^2+2x-8}$

   Vertical Asymptotes: _____

   Holes: _____

   Domain: _____

Determine the end behavior of each rational function.

3. $f(x) = \dfrac{x^2-4}{-3x}$

4. $f(x) = \dfrac{x^2+5x+6}{x^2+7x+12}$

_____   _____

Identify the asymptotes, holes, and *x*-intercepts of each rational function. Then graph the function.

5. $f(x) = \dfrac{x+2}{-2x^2-6x}$

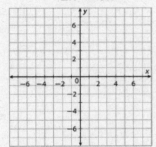

   Vertical Asymptotes: _____

   Horizontal Asymptotes: _____

   Holes: _____

   x-intercept(s): _____

6. $f(x) = \dfrac{-x^2+1}{x^2-3x+2}$

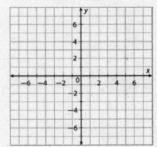

   Vertical Asymptotes: _____

   Horizontal Asymptotes: _____

   Holes: _____

   x-intercept(s): _____

LESSON 8-2

Graphing More Complicated Rational Functions

Practice and Problem Solving: C

Identify all vertical asymptotes and holes of each rational function. Then state its domain.

1. $f(x) = \dfrac{x^2 + 5x + 4}{-4x^2 + 4x + 24}$

   Vertical Asymptotes: _____

   Holes: _____

   Domain: _____

2. $f(x) = \dfrac{x^3 + 2x^2 - 3x}{-3x^2 - 12x - 9}$

   Vertical Asymptotes: _____

   Holes: _____

   Domain: _____

Determine the end behavior of each rational function.

3. $f(x) = \dfrac{x^2 - x - 2}{-3x}$

   _____

4. $f(x) = \dfrac{-3x^2 + 3x + 6}{x^2 - 2x - 3}$

   _____

Identify the asymptotes, holes, and *x*-intercepts of each rational function. Then graph the function.

5. $f(x) = \dfrac{-4x^2 + 4x}{x^3 - 5x^2 + 4x}$

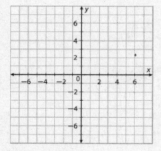

Vertical Asymptotes: _____

Horizontal Asymptotes: _____

Holes: _____

x-intercept(s): _____

6. $f(x) = \dfrac{x^3 - 9x}{x^3 - 7x^2 + 12x}$

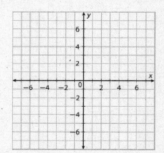

Vertical Asymptotes: _____

Horizontal Asymptotes: _____

Holes: _____

x-intercept(s): _____

LESSON 9-1

Adding and Subtracting Rational Expressions
Practice and Problem Solving: A/B

Identify the excluded values for each expression.

1. $\dfrac{x-7}{9x^2-63x}$

2. $\dfrac{x^2+3x-18}{-x^2+6x-9}$

_____   _____

Simplify the given expression stating any excluded values.

3. $\dfrac{2x^2-12x+16}{7x^2-28x}$

4. $\dfrac{5x^2+6x-8}{6x^2-24}$

_____   _____

5. $\dfrac{9x^3+9x^2}{7x^2-2x-9}$

6. $\dfrac{2x^2+13x-24}{7x+56}$

_____   _____

Add or subtract. Identify any *x*-values for which the expression is undefined.

7. $\dfrac{2x-3}{x+4}+\dfrac{4x-5}{x+4}$

8. $\dfrac{x+12}{2x-5}-\dfrac{3x-2}{2x-5}$

_____   _____

9. $\dfrac{x+4}{x^2-x-12}+\dfrac{2x}{x-4}$

10. $\dfrac{3x^2-1}{x^2-3x-18}-\dfrac{x+2}{x-6}$

_____   _____

11. $\dfrac{x+2}{x^2-2x-15}+\dfrac{x}{x+3}$

12. $\dfrac{x+6}{x^2-7x-18}-\dfrac{2x}{x-9}$

_____   _____

Solve.

13. A messenger is required to deliver 10 packages per day. Each day, the
    messenger works only for as long as it takes to deliver the daily quota
    of 10 packages. On average, the messenger is able to deliver 2
    packages per hour on Saturday and 4 packages per hour on Sunday.
    What is the messenger's average delivery rate on the weekend?

_____

LESSON	**Adding and Subtracting Rational Expressions**
9-1	*Practice and Problem Solving: C*

Identify the excluded values for each expression.

1. $\dfrac{7x^2 - 47x + 30}{3x^2 - 24x + 36}$

2. $\dfrac{2x^3 - 8x^2 - 64x}{5x^2 - 50x + 80}$

_____   _____

Simplify the given expression stating any excluded values.

3. $\dfrac{7x - 21}{15x^2 - 18x - 81}$

4. $\dfrac{6x^3 - 24x}{10x^3 + 2x^2 - 12x}$

_____   _____

5. $\dfrac{7x^2 - 14x + 7}{2x^2 - 4x + 2}$

6. $\dfrac{10x^3 + 60x^2}{15x^2 + 105x + 90}$

_____   _____

Add or subtract. Identify any *x*-values for which the expression is undefined.

7. $\dfrac{5x - 1}{x + 3} + \dfrac{3x}{2x + 6}$

8. $\dfrac{7x}{3x^2} - \dfrac{2}{x + 4}$

_____   _____

9. $\dfrac{x}{x - 4} + \dfrac{x + 1}{3x + 1}$

10. $\dfrac{3}{x - 5} - \dfrac{1}{x^2 - 7x + 10}$

_____   _____

11. $\dfrac{x}{4x - 2} + \dfrac{3x + 3}{4x + 2}$

12. $\dfrac{3x}{x^2 - x - 6} - \dfrac{5}{x^2 - 8x + 15}$

_____   _____

Solve.

13. The electric potential generated by a certain arrangement of electric charges is given by $\dfrac{e}{x - 4} + \dfrac{e}{x + 1}$, where *e* is the fundamental unit of electric charge and *x* measures the location where the potential is being measured. Express the electric potential as a rational expression.

_____

LESSON 9-2
Multiplying and Dividing Rational Expressions
Practice and Problem Solving: A/B

Multiply. State any excluded values.

1. $\dfrac{6x}{10} \cdot \dfrac{6x}{3x^3}$

_____

2. $\dfrac{4x}{3} \cdot \dfrac{8x}{2}$

_____

3. $\dfrac{1}{x+9} \cdot \dfrac{7x^3 + 49x^2}{x+7}$

_____

4. $\dfrac{6x^2 - 54x}{x-9} \cdot \dfrac{7x}{6x}$

_____

5. $\dfrac{18x - 36}{4x - 8} \cdot \dfrac{2}{9x + 18}$

_____

6. $\left(56 + 11x - 15x^2\right) \cdot \dfrac{10}{15x^2 - 11x - 56}$

_____

Divide. State any excluded values.

7. $\dfrac{4x}{5x} \div \dfrac{4x}{6}$

_____

8. $\dfrac{6(x-2)}{(x-1)(x-10)} \div \dfrac{x-2}{x-10}$

_____

9. $(2x + 6) \div \dfrac{14x^2 + 42x}{10}$

_____

10. $\dfrac{27x + 9}{10} \div \dfrac{3x^2 - 8x - 3}{10}$

_____

11. $\dfrac{24x + 56}{10x^3 - 90x^2} \div \dfrac{15x + 35}{5}$

_____

12. $\dfrac{2x + 20}{12x^3 - 30x^2} \div \dfrac{2}{14x - 35}$

_____

Solve.

13. The distance, *d*, traveled by a car undergoing constant acceleration, *a*,

    for a time, *t*, is given by $d = v_0 t + \dfrac{1}{2}at^2$, where v_0 is the initial velocity of

    the car. Two cars are side by side with the same initial velocity. One
    car accelerates, $a = A$, and the other car does not accelerate, $a = 0$.
    Write an expression for the ratio of the distance traveled by the
    accelerating car to the distance traveled by the nonaccelerating car as
    a function of time.

    _____

LESSON 9-2

Multiplying and Dividing Rational Expressions

Practice and Problem Solving: C

Multiply. State any excluded values.

1. $\dfrac{27x}{19x} \cdot \dfrac{12x^4}{11}$

_____

2. $\dfrac{14x^2}{15x} \cdot \dfrac{41x}{49}$

_____

3. $\dfrac{169x^2 + 104x - 48}{44x^3} \cdot \dfrac{x - 11}{169x^2 + 104x - 48}$

_____

4. $\dfrac{3x + 5}{15x^2 + 34x + 15} \cdot \dfrac{5x^2 - 62x - 39}{5x^2 - 50x}$

_____

5. $\dfrac{5x - 8}{2x^2 + 14x + 20} \cdot \dfrac{20x^2 + 40x}{15x^2 - 24x}$

_____

6. $\dfrac{15x^2 + 12x}{40x + 32} \cdot \dfrac{7x - 14}{3x}$

_____

Divide. State any excluded values.

7. $\dfrac{14x^2}{6x^3} \div \dfrac{7}{3x}$

_____

8. $\dfrac{5(x + 13)}{x + 13} \div \dfrac{5x - 30}{14x^2}$

_____

9. $\dfrac{84x^2}{7x + 10} \div \dfrac{11x + 132}{77x + 110}$

_____

10. $\dfrac{2x^2 + 10x - 12}{22x^2 - 42x + 20} \div \dfrac{1}{11x^2 + 100x - 100}$

_____

11. $\dfrac{77x + 11}{3x - 42} \div \dfrac{21x + 3}{3}$

_____

12. $\dfrac{7x - 4}{-91x^2 + 108x - 32} \div \dfrac{x^2 + 4x - 5}{13x^2 + 109x - 72}$

_____

Solve.

13. The formula for the volume of a cylinder is $\pi r^2 h$ and the formula for its surface area is $2\pi r^2 + 2\pi rh$, where r is the radius and h is the height. A cylindrical industrial storage tank has a surface area-to-volume ratio of 3. If the height of the cylindrical tank is 2 meters, what is the radius?

_____

LESSON 9-3

Solving Rational Equations

Practice and Problem Solving: A/B

Identify any excluded values. Rewrite the equation with 0 on one side. Then graph to find the solution.

1. $-\dfrac{2}{x-3}=2$

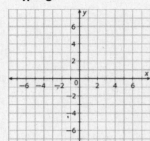

_____

2. $\dfrac{4}{x-2}=-2$

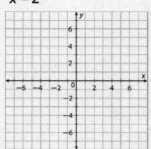

_____

Find the LCD for each pair.

3. $\dfrac{13}{4x}$ and $\dfrac{27}{3x^2}$

_____

4. $\dfrac{11}{x^2+3x+2}$ and $\dfrac{1}{x+2}$

_____

Solve each equation algebraically.

5. $\dfrac{1}{x}-\dfrac{x-2}{3x}=\dfrac{4}{3x}$

_____

6. $\dfrac{5x-5}{x^2-4x}-\dfrac{5}{x^2-4x}=\dfrac{1}{x}$

_____

7. $\dfrac{x^2-7x+10}{x}+\dfrac{1}{x}=x+4$

_____

8. $\dfrac{4}{x^2-4}=\dfrac{1}{x-2}$

_____

Solve.

9. The time required to deliver and install a computer at a customer's location is $t=4+\dfrac{d}{r}$, where t is time in hours, d is the distance, in miles, from the warehouse to the customer's location, and r is the average speed of the delivery truck. If it takes 6.2 hours for the employee to deliver and install a computer for a customer located 100 miles from the warehouse, what is the average speed of the delivery truck?

_____

LESSON
9-3

Solving Rational Equations

Practice and Problem Solving: C

Identify any excluded values. Rewrite the equation with 0 on one side. Then graph to find the solution.

1. $12 = \dfrac{2}{x-3} + 14$

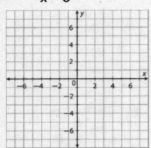

2. $\dfrac{3}{x-1} - 16 = -16$

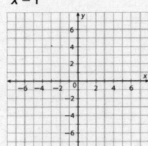

_____

_____

Find the LCD for each pair.

3. $\dfrac{7}{3x^2y^6}$ and $\dfrac{23}{5x^3y^2}$

4. $\dfrac{17}{x^2+x-2}$ and $\dfrac{5x}{x^2-x-6}$

_____

_____

Solve each equation algebraically.

5. $-\dfrac{6}{x} + 1 = \dfrac{7}{x^2}$

6. $\dfrac{4x}{x-4} = \dfrac{2x+8}{x-4}$

_____

_____

7. $1 + \dfrac{x}{x+3} = \dfrac{x^2-8x+12}{2x^2+13x+21}$

8. $\dfrac{x^2+7x+10}{5x-30} + \dfrac{x}{x-6} = \dfrac{x^2-13x+40}{5x-30}$

_____

_____

Solve.

9. An artist is designing a picture frame whose length *l* and width *w*

   satisfy the Golden Ratio, which is $\dfrac{w}{l} = \dfrac{l}{l+w}$. If the length of the frame

   is 24 inches, what is the width of the frame?

_____

_____

LESSON 10-1

Inverses of Simple Quadratic and Cubic Functions

Practice and Problem Solving: A/B

Graph the function $f(x)$ for the domain $x \geq 0$. Then graph its inverse, $f^{-1}(x)$, and write a rule for the inverse function.

1. $f(x) = 0.25x^2$

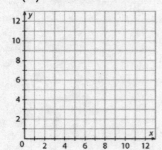

_____

2. $f(x) = x^2 + 3$

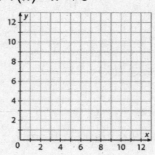

_____

Graph the function $f(x)$. Then graph its inverse, $f^{-1}(x)$, and write a rule for the inverse function.

3. $f(x) = 0.5x^3$

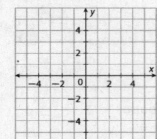

_____

4. $f(x) = x^3 - 2$

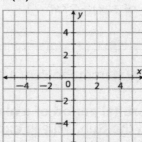

_____

The function $d = 4.9t^2$ gives the distance, d, in meters, that an object dropped from a height will fall in t seconds. Use this for Problems 5–6.

5. Express t as a function of d.

_____

6. Find the number of seconds it takes an object to fall 150 feet. Round to the nearest tenth of a second.

_____

LESSON 10-1

Inverses of Simple Quadratic and Cubic Functions

Practice and Problem Solving: C

Solve. Assume the domain is restricted to $\{x \mid x \geq 0\}$.

1. Find the inverse of $f(x) = \dfrac{1}{10}x^2$.

   _____

2. Find the inverse of $f(x) = 2x^2 - 7$.

   _____

3. Graph $f(x)$ and $f^{-1}(x)$ from Problem 1.

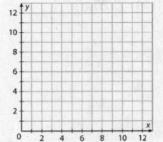

Solve.

4. Find the inverse of $f(x) = 0.125x^3$.

   _____

5. Find the inverse of $f(x) = 27x^3 - 1$.

   _____

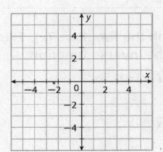

6. Graph $f(x)$ and $f^{-1}(x)$ from Problem 4.

The square of the orbital period of a planet is proportional to the cube of its distance from the Sun. This is expressed in the formula $T^2 = a^3$, where T is time, measured in years, and a is distance, measured in astronomical units (1 astronomical unit is the mean distance of Earth from the Sun). Use this information for Problems 7–9.

7. Express a as a function of T. Express T as a function of a.

   _____

8. Pluto's orbital period is approximately 247.9 times that of Earth's. Estimate Pluto's mean distance from the Sun. Show your work.

   _____

9. Venus's mean distance from the Sun is approximately 72.3% that of Earth's. Estimate Venus's orbital period. Show your work.

   _____

**LESSON
10-2**
Graphing Square Root Functions
Practice and Problem Solving: A/B

Graph each function, and identify its domain and range.

1. $f(x) = \sqrt{x-4}$

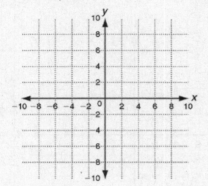

Domain: _____

Range: _____

2. $f(x) = 2\sqrt{x} + 1$

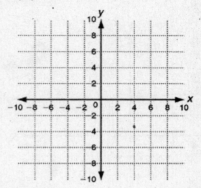

Domain: _____

Range: _____

Using the graph of $f(x) = \sqrt{x}$ as a guide, describe the transformation.

3. $g(x) = 4\sqrt{x+8}$ _____

4. $g(x) = -\sqrt{3x} + 2$ _____

Use the description to write the square root function g.

5. The parent function $f(x) = \sqrt{x}$ is reflected across
the y-axis, vertically stretched by a factor of 7, and

translated 3 units down.   _____

6. The parent function $f(x) = \sqrt{x}$ is translated 2 units right,

compressed horizontally by a factor of $\dfrac{1}{2}$, and reflected

across the x-axis.   _____

Solve.

7. The radius, r, of a cylinder can be found using the function $r = \sqrt{\dfrac{V}{\pi h}}$, where

V is the volume and h is the height of the cylinder.

a. Find the radius of a cylinder with a volume of 200 cubic
inches and a height of 4 inches. Use $\pi = 3.14$. Round to
the nearest hundredth.   _____

b. The volume of a cylinder is doubled without changing
its height. How did its radius change? Explain your
reasoning.   _____

LESSON 10-2

Graphing Square Root Functions

Practice and Problem Solving: C

Graph each function, and identify its domain and range.

1. $g(x) = \frac{1}{2}\sqrt{-x} - 3$

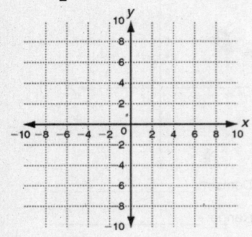

Domain: _____

Range: _____

2. $g(x) = -4\sqrt{x+2} + 6$

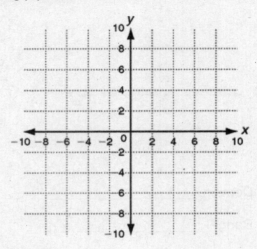

Domain: _____

Range: _____

Use the description to write the square root function g.

3. The parent function $f(x) = \sqrt{x}$ is compressed vertically

by a factor of $\frac{1}{4}$, reflected across the x-axis, and

translated 6 units up.   _____

4. The parent function $f(x) = \sqrt{x}$ is translated 8 units left,

reflected across the y-axis, and stretched horizontally

by a factor of 3.   _____

Solve.

5. The frequency, *f*, in Hz, at which a simple pendulum rocks back and forth is given

by $f = \frac{1}{2\pi}\sqrt{\frac{g}{l}}$, where *g* is the strength of the gravitational field at the location

of the pendulum, and *l* is the length of the pendulum.

a. Find the frequency of a pendulum whose length
   is 1 foot and where the gravitational field is
   approximately 32 ft/s².   _____

b. The strength of the gravitational field on the moon is

   about $\frac{1}{6}$ as strong as on Earth. Find the frequency

   of the same pendulum on the moon.   _____

LESSON 10-3

Graphing Cube Root Functions

Practice and Problem Solving: A/B

Graph each cube root function. Then describe the graph as a transformation of the graph of the parent function. (The graph of the parent function is shown.)

1. $g(x) = \sqrt[3]{x-3} + 2$

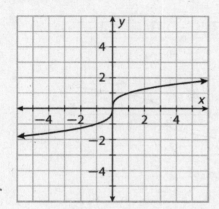

_____

2. $g(x) = \frac{1}{2}\sqrt[3]{x+2} - 3$

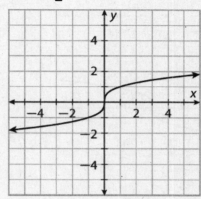

_____

Write the equation of the cube root function shown on the graph.
Use the form $g(x) = a\sqrt[3]{x-h} + k$.

3.

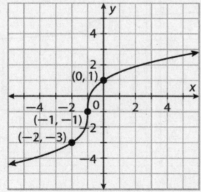

_____

4.

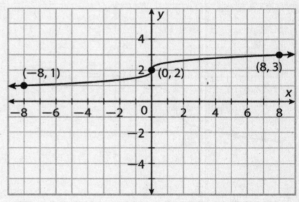

_____

Write an equation, $g(x)$, for the transformation equation described.

5. The graph of $f(x) = \sqrt[3]{x}$ is reflected across the y-axis and then translated 4 units down and 12 units to the left.

_____

6. The graph of $f(x) = \sqrt[3]{x}$ is stretched vertically by a factor of 8, reflected across the x-axis, and then translated 11 units to the right.

_____

LESSON 10-3

Graphing Cube Root Functions

Practice and Problem Solving: C

Graph each cube root function. Then describe the graph as a transformation of the graph of the parent function. (The graph of the parent function is shown.)

1. $g(x) = -2.5\sqrt[3]{x+2} + 1.5$

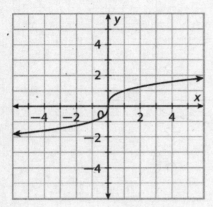

2. $g(x) = \sqrt[3]{-2x-4} - \dfrac{1}{2}$

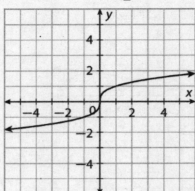

_____

_____

Write the equation of the cube root function shown on the graph.

3.

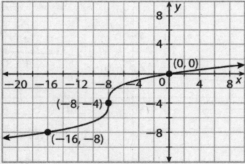

4.

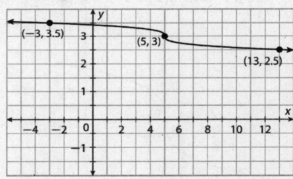

_____

_____

Write an equation, $g(x)$, for the transformation equation described.

5. The graph of the function $f(x) = 7\sqrt[3]{x-4} + 3$ is translated 2 units to the left and then 4 units up.

_____

6. The graph of the function $f(x) = -\sqrt[3]{x+2} - 5$ is vertically stretched by a factor of 3, translated 2 units to the right, and then reflected across the x-axis.

_____

LESSON 11-1

Radical Expressions and Rational Exponents
Practice and Problem Solving: A/B

Write each expression in radical form. Simplify numerical expressions when possible.

1. $64^{\frac{5}{6}}$

_____

2. $(6x)^{\frac{3}{2}}$

_____

3. $(-8)^{\frac{4}{3}}$

_____

4. $(5r^3)^{\frac{1}{4}}$

_____

5. $27^{\frac{2}{3}}$

_____

6. $(100a)^{\frac{1}{2}}$

_____

7. $10^{\frac{8}{5}}$

_____

8. $(x^2)^{\frac{2}{5}}$

_____

9. $(7x)^{-\frac{1}{3}}$

_____

Write each expression by using rational exponents. Simplify numerical expressions when possible.

10. $\left(\sqrt[4]{2}\right)^7$

_____

11. $\left(\sqrt{5x}\right)^3$

_____

12. $\sqrt[5]{51^4}$

_____

13. $\left(\sqrt{169}\right)^3$

_____

14. $\left(\sqrt[4]{2v}\right)^3$

_____

15. $\left(\sqrt[5]{n^2}\right)^2$

_____

16. $\dfrac{1}{\left(\sqrt{3m}\right)^3}$

_____

17. $\sqrt[7]{36^{14}}$

_____

18. $\dfrac{1}{\left(\sqrt[4]{5p}\right)^7}$

_____

Solve.

19. In every atom, electrons orbit the nucleus with a certain characteristic velocity known as the Fermi-Thomas velocity, equal to $\dfrac{Z^{\frac{2}{3}}}{137}c$, where Z is the number of protons in the nucleus and c is the speed of light. In terms of c, what is the characteristic Fermi-Thomas velocity of the electrons in Uranium, for which $Z = 92$?

_____

LESSON
11-1
Radical Expressions and Rational Exponents
Practice and Problem Solving: C

Write each expression in radical form. Simplify numerical expressions when possible.

1. $216^{\frac{2}{3}}$

2. $\left(121m^2\right)^{\frac{1}{3}}$

3. $\left(27x\right)^{\frac{5}{3}}$

_____ _____ _____

4. $\left(10b\right)^{2.5}$

5. $1000^{-\frac{2}{3}}$

6. $\left(37x^2\right)^{-\frac{1}{6}}$

_____ _____ _____

7. $\left(16x^3\right)^{\frac{3}{2}}$

8. $\left(5x\right)^{-1.25}$

9. $\left(162r^2\right)^{\frac{1}{4}}$

_____ _____ _____

Write each expression by using rational exponents. Simplify numerical expressions when possible.

10. $\left(\sqrt[19]{19n}\right)^2$

11. $\sqrt[5]{\left(3^5 x\right)^3}$

12. $\left(\sqrt[4]{181x^4}\right)^3$

_____ _____ _____

13. $\dfrac{1}{\left(\sqrt{5n}\right)^5}$

14. $\left(\sqrt{4x^3 y^5}\right)^3$

15. $\left(\sqrt[5]{-6}\right)^3$

_____ _____ _____

16. $\left(\sqrt[3]{27x^3 y^6}\right)^2$

17. $\sqrt[4]{30x^3}$

18. $\dfrac{1}{\left(\sqrt[3]{8a}\right)^5}$

_____ _____ _____

Solve.

19. Each key on a piano produces a frequency that is $2^{\frac{1}{12}}$ times higher than the frequency of the key immediately to its left. Moving *n* keys to the right of any key increases the frequency of the starting note by a factor $2^{\frac{n}{12}}$. The key corresponding to Concert A has a frequency of 440 Hz. What is the frequency of note D, which is 5 keys to the right of Concert A?

_____

Simplifying Radical Expressions

LESSON 11-2

Practice and Problem Solving: A/B

Simplify each expression. Assume all variables are positive.

1. $-3\sqrt{12r}$

2. $4^{\frac{3}{2}} \cdot 4^{\frac{5}{2}}$

3. $\dfrac{27^{\frac{4}{3}}}{27^{\frac{2}{3}}}$

4. $\dfrac{\left(a^2\right)^2}{a^{\frac{3}{2}}b^{\frac{1}{2}} \cdot b}$

5. $(27 \cdot 64)^{\frac{2}{3}}$

6. $\left(\dfrac{1}{243}\right)^{\frac{1}{5}}$

7. $\dfrac{(25x)^{\frac{3}{2}}}{5x^{\frac{1}{2}}}$

8. $(4x)^{-\frac{1}{2}} \cdot (9x)^{\frac{1}{2}}$

9. $3\sqrt[3]{81x^4y^2}$

10. $-5\sqrt[3]{-500x^5y^3}$

Solve.

11. The frequency, *f*, in Hz, at which a simple pendulum rocks back and

forth is given by $f = \dfrac{1}{2\pi}\sqrt{\dfrac{g}{l}}$, where *g* is the strength of the gravitational

field at the location of the pendulum, and *l* is the length of the pendulum.

a. Rewrite the formula so that it gives the length *l* of the pendulum in terms of *g* and *f*. Then simplify the formula using the fact that the gravitational field is approximately 32 ft/s².

b. Use the equation found in part a to find the length of a pendulum, to the nearest foot, that has a frequency of 0.52 Hz.

Simplifying Radical Expressions
Practice and Problem Solving: C

Simplify each expression. Assume all variables are positive.

1. $\left(x^{\frac{1}{2}} \cdot x^{\frac{1}{2}} y^{\frac{3}{2}}\right)^2$

2. $\left(\left(r^{\frac{7}{4}}\right)^{\frac{1}{4}} \cdot r\right)^2$

3. $\left(\dfrac{x^8}{y^4}\right)^{\frac{3}{4}}$

4. $\left(\dfrac{x^3}{125}\right)^{\frac{1}{3}}$

5. $\left(-8x^{18}\right)^{\frac{2}{3}}\left(\sqrt[3]{y^6}\right)$

6. $\dfrac{x^{-2}y^2 \cdot y^2}{\left(x^{-\frac{1}{2}}\right)^{-\frac{1}{2}} \cdot \left(x^{-1}y^{-2}\right)^{-1}}$

7. $\left(\sqrt[3]{-8x^9}\right)^2$

8. $(3x)^{\frac{2}{3}}(3x)^{\frac{7}{3}}$

9. $\left(\dfrac{m^8}{n^{12}}\right)^{-\frac{1}{4}}$

10. $5\sqrt[3]{-750u^5v^5}$

Solve.

11. Rafael is renting a cube-shaped bounce house for a party. The area in his yard he has marked off for the bounce house is 462.25 square feet.

    a. The rental company is able to provide Rafael with volumes of its various bounce houses. Rafael wants to know the area of a side. Use rational exponents to write a formula that Rafael could use to find the area of one side of the bounce house given its volume.

    b. The bounce house Rafael likes best has a volume of 9261 ft³. What area of ground will the bounce house cover in square feet? Will the bounce house fit in the spot he has marked off? Show your work.

LESSON 11-3
Solving Radical Equations
Practice and Problem Solving: A/B

Solve each equation.

1. $\sqrt{x+6} = 7$

_____

2. $\sqrt{5x} = 10$

_____

3. $\sqrt{2x+5} = \sqrt{3x-1}$

_____

4. $\sqrt{x+4} = 3\sqrt{x}$

_____

5. $\sqrt[3]{x-6} = \sqrt[3]{3x+24}$

_____

6. $3\sqrt[3]{x} = \sqrt[3]{7x+5}$

_____

7. $\sqrt{-14x+2} = x-3$

_____

8. $(x+4)^{\frac{1}{2}} = 6$

_____

9. $4(x-3)^{\frac{1}{2}} = 8$

_____

10. $4(x-12)^{\frac{1}{3}} = -16$

_____

11. $\sqrt{3x+6} = 3$

_____

12. $\sqrt{x-4} + 3 = 9$

_____

13. $\sqrt{x+7} = \sqrt{2x-1}$

_____

14. $\sqrt{2x-7} = 2x$

_____

Solve.

15. A biologist is studying two species of animals in a habitat. The population, p_1, of one of the species is growing according to $p_1 = 500t^{\frac{3}{2}}$ and the population, p_2, of the other species is growing according to $p_2 = 100t^2$, where time, t, is measured in years. After how many years will the populations of the two species be equal?

_____

LESSON
11-3

Solving Radical Equations

Practice and Problem Solving: C

Solve each equation.

1. $\sqrt[3]{4x+1} - 5 = 0$

_____

2. $3\sqrt{x-11} = 18$

_____

3. $\sqrt[4]{10x+11} = 3$

_____

4. $\sqrt[3]{3x} = \sqrt[3]{2x+9}$

_____

5. $x + 2 = \sqrt{3x+6}$

_____

6. $(10x-25)^{\frac{1}{2}} = x$

_____

7. $5(6x+1)^{\frac{1}{4}} = 10$

_____

8. $4(7x+18)^{\frac{1}{2}} = 4x$

_____

9. $\sqrt{4x+5} = 3$

_____

10. $\sqrt[3]{x+3} = 2$

_____

11. $\sqrt{x-7} + 9 = 12$

_____

12. $\sqrt[3]{x-6} + 7 = 4$

_____

13. $\sqrt{3x-1} = \sqrt{x+7}$

_____

14. $\sqrt[3]{x+2} - 1 = 4$

_____

Solve.

15. Einstein's theory of relativity states that the mass of an object increases as the object's velocity increases. The mass, $m(v)$, of an object traveling with velocity, v, is given by $m(v) = \dfrac{m_0}{\sqrt{1-\dfrac{v^2}{c^2}}}$, where c is the speed of light and m_0 is the mass of the object at rest. In terms of c, solve for the velocity at which the effective mass, $m(v)$, of the particle has increased to twice its mass at rest, m_0.

_____

LESSON 12-1

Arithmetic Sequences

Practice and Problem Solving: A/B

Write an explicit rule and a recursive rule for each sequence.

1.

n	1	2	3	4	5
$f(n)$	8	12	16	20	24

_____

_____

2.

n	1	2	3	4	5
$f(n)$	11	7	3	−1	−5

_____

_____

3.

n	1	2	3	4	5
$f(n)$	−20	−13	−6	1	8

_____

_____

4.

n	1	2	3	4	5
$f(n)$	2.7	4.3	5.9	7.5	9.1

_____

_____

5.

n	1	2	3	4	5
$f(n)$	1	−8	−17	−26	−35

_____

_____

6.

n	1	2	3	4	5
$f(n)$	−3	2.5	8	13.5	19

_____

_____

Solve.

7. The explicit rule for an arithmetic sequence is $f(n) = 13 + 6(n − 1)$. Find the first four terms of the sequence.

_____

8. Helene paid back $100 in Month 1 of her loan. In each month after that, she paid back $50. Write an explicit formula and a recursive formula that shows $f(n)$, the total amount Helene had paid back by Month n.

_____

9. The explicit rule for an arithmetic sequence is $f(n) = 18 + 5(n − 1)$. Write a recursive rule for this sequence.

_____

10. A recursive rule for an arithmetic sequence is $f(1) = 7$, $f(n) = f(n − 1) + 47$ for $n \geq 2$. Write an explicit rule for this sequence.

_____

LESSON 12-1
Arithmetic Sequences
Practice and Problem Solving: C

Write an explicit rule and a recursive rule for each sequence.

1.

n	1	2	3	4	5
$f(n)$	−3.4	−2.1	−0.8	0.5	1.8

_____

_____

2.

n	1	2	3	4	5
$f(n)$	$\frac{1}{6}$	$\frac{1}{4}$	$\frac{1}{3}$	$\frac{5}{12}$	$\frac{1}{2}$

_____

_____

3.

n	1	3	5	6	9
$f(n)$	82	81	80	79.5	78

_____

_____

4.

n	1	4	8	13	19
$f(n)$	−22	2	34	74	122

_____

_____

Solve.

5. A recursive rule for an arithmetic sequence is $f(1) = -8$, $f(n) = f(n - 1) - 6.5$ for $n \geq 2$. Write an explicit rule for this sequence.

_____

6. The third and thirtieth terms of an arithmetic sequence are 4 and 85. Write an explicit rule for this sequence.

_____

7. $f(n) = 900 - 60(n - 1)$ represents the amount Oscar still needs to repay on a loan at the beginning of Month n. Find the amount Oscar pays monthly and the month in which he will make his last payment.

_____

8. Find the first six terms of the sequence whose explicit formula is $f(n) = (-1)^n$. Explain whether it is an arithmetic sequence.

_____

9. An arithmetic sequence has common difference of 5.6, and its tenth term is 75. Write a recursive formula for this sequence.

_____

10. The cost of a college's annual tuition follows an arithmetic sequence. The cost was $35,000 in 2010 and $40,000 in 2012. According to this sequence, what will tuition be in 2020?

_____

LESSON 12-2

Geometric Sequences

Practice and Problem Solving: A/B

Each rule represents a geometric sequence. If the given rule is recursive, write it as an explicit rule. If the rule is explicit, write it as a recursive rule. Assume that $f(1)$ is the first term of the sequence.

1. $f(n) = 11(2)^{n-1}$

2. $f(1) = 2.5; f(n) = f(n-1) \cdot 3.5$ for $n \geq 2$

_____

_____

3. $f(1) = 27; f(n) = f(n-1) \cdot \dfrac{1}{3}$ for $n \geq 2$

4. $f(n) = -4(0.5)^{n-1}$

_____

_____

Write an explicit rule for each geometric sequence based on the given terms from the sequence. Assume that the common ratio r is positive.

5. $a_1 = 90$ and $a_2 = 360$

6. $a_1 = 16$ and $a_3 = 4$

_____

_____

7. $a_1 = 2$ and $a_5 = 162$

8. $a_2 = 30$ and $a_3 = 10$

_____

_____

9. $a_4 = 135$ and $a_5 = 405$

10. $a_3 = 400$ and $a_5 = 256$

_____

_____

11. $a_2 = 80$ and $a_5 = 10$

12. $a_4 = 22$ and $a_7 = 0.022$

_____

_____

A bank account earns a constant rate of interest each month. The account was opened on March 1 with $18,000 in it. On April 1, the balance in the account was $18,045. Use this information for Problems 13–15.

13. Write an explicit rule and a recursive rule that can be used to find $A(n)$, the balance after n months.

_____

14. Find the balance after 5 months.

_____

15. Find the balance after 5 years.

_____

LESSON
12-2

Geometric Sequences

Practice and Problem Solving: C

Each rule represents a geometric sequence. If the given rule is recursive, write it as an explicit rule. If the rule is explicit, write it as a recursive rule. Assume that $f(1)$ is the first term of the sequence.

1. $f(1) = \dfrac{2}{3}$; $f(n) = f(n-1) \cdot 8$ for $n \geq 2$

2. $f(n) = -10(0.4)^{n-1}$

_____   _____

Write an explicit rule for each geometric sequence based on the given terms from the sequence. Assume that the common ratio r is positive.

3. $a_1 = 6$ and $a_4 = 162$

4. $a_2 = 9$ and $a_4 = 2.25$

_____   _____

5. $a_4 = 0.01$ and $a_5 = 0.0001$

6. $a_3 = \dfrac{1}{48}$ and $a_4 = \dfrac{1}{192}$

_____   _____

7. $a_3 = 32$ and $a_6 = \dfrac{256}{125}$

8. $a_2 = -4$ and $a_4 = -9$

_____   _____

Solve.

9. A geometric sequence contains the terms $a_3 = 40$ and $a_5 = 640$.
   Write the explicit rules for $r > 0$ and for $r < 0$.

_____

10. The sum of the first n terms of the geometric sequence $f(n) = ar^{n-1}$ can
    be found using the formula $\dfrac{a(r^n - 1)}{r - 1}$. Use this formula to find the sum
    $1 + 3 + 3^2 + 3^3 + \ldots + 3^{10}$. Check your answer the long way.

_____

11. An account earning interest compounded annually was worth $44,100
    after 2 years and $48,620.25 after 4 years. What is the interest rate?

_____

12. There are 64 teams in a basketball tournament. All teams play in the
    first round but only winning teams move on to subsequent rounds.
    Write an explicit rule for $T(n)$, the number of games in the nth round of
    the tournament. State the domain of the rule.

_____

LESSON 12-3

Geometric Series

Practice and Problem Solving: A/B

Determine the values of *a*, *n*, and *r* for each geometric series. Then use the summation formula to find the sum.

1. $1 + 6 + 36 + 216 + 1296$

_____

_____

2. $2 - 12 + 72 - 432$

_____

_____

3. $-1 - 4 - 16 - 64 - 256$

_____

_____

4. $-4 + 8 - 16 + 32 - 64$

_____

_____

Determine the number of terms in each geometric series. Then evaluate the sum.

5. $3 + 15 + 75 + ... + 46{,}875$

_____

_____

6. $2 - 6 + 18 - ... + 1458$

_____

_____

7. $-1 - 5 - 25 - ... - 78{,}125$

_____

_____

8. $-4 - 16 - 64 - ... - 262{,}144$

_____

_____

Evaluate each geometric series described.

9. A geometric series begins with 4, ends with $\dfrac{1}{64}$, and has terms that decrease successively by half.

_____

10. A geometric series has 9 terms, starts with –2, and has a common ratio of –4.

_____

Solve.

11. Deanna received an e-mail asking her to forward it to 10 other people. Assume that no one breaks the chain and that there are no duplicate recipients. How many e-mails will have been sent after 8 generations, including Deanna's?

_____

LESSON
12-3

Geometric Series

Practice and Problem Solving: C

Determine the values of *a*, *n*, and *r* for each geometric series. Then use the summation formula to find the sum.

1. $1.25 + 5 + 20 + 80 + 320$

_____

_____

2. $-2 + 10 - 50 + 250 - 1250$

_____

_____

3. $2 + 1 + \dfrac{1}{2} + \dfrac{1}{4}$

_____

_____

4. $-20 - 10 - 5 - \dfrac{5}{2} - \dfrac{5}{4}$

_____

_____

Evaluate the sum.

5. $-2.5 - 5 - 10 - \ldots - 160$

_____

6. $-64 + 32 - 16 + \ldots - 0.25$

_____

7. $1 - \dfrac{1}{4} + \dfrac{1}{16} - \ldots - \dfrac{1}{262,144}$

_____

8. $2 + 1 + \dfrac{1}{2} + \ldots + \dfrac{1}{256}$

_____

Evaluate each geometric series described.

9. A geometric series begins with –2, ends with $-\dfrac{4374}{78,125}$, and has terms that decrease successively by 40%.

_____

10. A geometric series has 9 terms that start with $-\dfrac{7}{5}$ and have a common ratio of $\dfrac{1}{2}$.

_____

Solve.

11. Miguel paid $9600 in rent for his apartment the first year. Every year for the next 3 years the rent increased 5%.

   a. How much rent did he pay in the fourth year? _____

   b. How much rent did he pay altogether in the 4 years? _____

Name _____ Date _____ Class_____

Exponential Growth Functions
Practice and Problem Solving: A/B

Use two points to write an equation for each function shown.

1.
x	0	1	2	3
f(x)	6	18	54	162

2.
x	−4	−2	0	2	4
f(x)	−2.98	−2.75	−2	1	13

_____   _____

Graph each function.

3. $y = 5(2)^x$

4. $y = -2(3)^x$

5. $y = \dfrac{1}{2}(2)^{x-1} + 3$

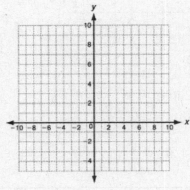
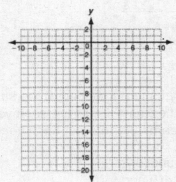
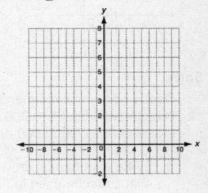

Solve.

6. The annual sales for a fast food restaurant are $650,000 and are increasing at a rate of 4% per year. Write the function $f(n)$ that expresses the annual sales after n years. Then find the annual sales after 5 years.

_____

7. Starting with 25 members, a club doubled its membership every year. Write the function $f(n)$ that expresses the number of members in the club after n years. Then find the number of members after 6 years.

_____

8. During a certain period of time, about 70 northern sea otters had an annual growth rate of 18%. Write the function $f(n)$ that expresses the population of sea otters after n years. Then find the population of sea otters after 4 years.

_____

**LESSON
13-1**

Exponential Growth Functions

Practice and Problem Solving: C

Graph each function. On your graph, include points to indicate the ordered pairs for $x = -1, 0, 1,$ and 2.

1. $f(x) = 0.75(2)^x$

2. $f(x) = 6(3)^{x-1}$

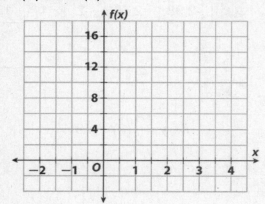

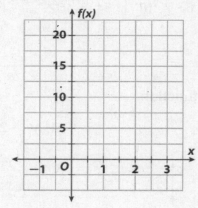

Solve.

3. Odette has two investments that she purchased at the same time. Investment 1 cost $10,000 and earns 4% interest each year. Investment 2 cost $8000 and earns 6% interest each year.

   a. Write exponential growth functions that could be used to find $v_1(t)$ and $v_2(t)$, _____

   the values of the investments after t years. _____

   b. Find the value of each investment after 5 years. Explain why the difference between their values, _____

   which was initially $2000, is now less. _____

4. If A is deposited in a bank account at r% annual interest, compounded annually, its value at the end of n years $V(n)$ can be found using the

   formula $V(n) = A\left(1 + \dfrac{r}{100}\right)^n$. Suppose that $5000 is invested in an

   account paying 4% interest. Find its value after 10 years.

   _____

5. The graph of $f(x) = 6(3)^{x-1}$ from Problem 2 moves closer and closer

   to the x-axis as x decreases. Does the graph ever reach the x-axis? Explain your reasoning and what your conclusion implies about the range of the function.

   _____

   _____

LESSON
13-2

Exponential Decay Functions

Practice and Problem Solving: A/B

Use two points to write an equation for each function shown.

1.

x	0	1	2	3
f(x)	36	27	20.25	15.1875

2.

x	−2	0	2	4
f(x)	84	21	5.25	1.3125

_____   _____

Graph each function.

3. $y = \left(\dfrac{1}{2}\right)^x - 3$

4. $y = -(0.5)^{x+3} - 3$

5. $y = 3\left(\dfrac{1}{2}\right)^x$

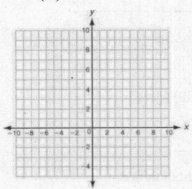
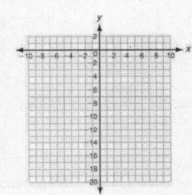
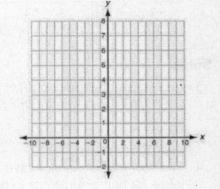

Solve.

6. If a basketball is bounced from a height of 15 feet, the function
$f(x) = 15(0.75)^x$ gives the height of the ball in feet of each bounce,
where x is the bounce number. What will be the height of the 5th
bounce? Round to the nearest tenth of a foot.

_____

7. The value of a company's equipment is $25,000 and decreases at a
rate of 15% per year. Write the function, $f(n)$, that expresses the value
of the equipment after n years. Then find the value of the equipment in
year eight.

_____

8. In 1995, the population of a town was 33,500. It is decreasing at a rate
of 2.5% per decade. Write the function, $f(n)$, that expresses the
population of the town after n decades. What is the expected
population of the town in the year 2025 to the nearest hundred?

_____

LESSON 13-2

Exponential Decay Functions

Practice and Problem Solving: C

Graph each function. On your graph, include points to indicate the ordered pairs for x = –1, 0, 1, and 2.

1. $f(x) = 5(0.4)^x + 1$

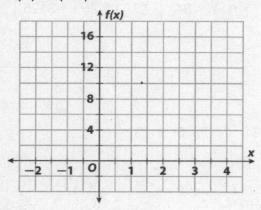

2. $f(x) = -15(0.3)^{x+1} + 20$

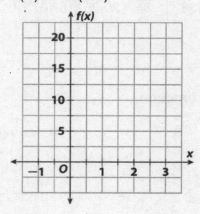

Solve.

3. An exponential function $f(x)$ passes through the points (2, 360) and (3, 216). Write an equation for $f(x)$.

_____

4. The half-life of a radioactive substance is the average amount of time it takes for half of its atoms to decay. Suppose you started with 200 grams of a substance with a half-life of 3 minutes. How many minutes have passed if 25 grams now remain? Explain your reasoning.

_____

_____

5. Colleen's office equipment is depreciating at a rate of 9% per year. She paid $24,500 for it in 2009. Write the function $f(n)$ that expresses the value of the equipment after n years. What will the equipment be worth in 2015 to the nearest hundred dollars?

_____

6. A car depreciates in value by 20% each year. Graham argued that the value of the car after 5 years must be $0, since 20% • 5 = 100%. Do you agree or disagree? Explain fully.

_____

_____

LESSON 13-3

The Base e

Practice and Problem Solving: A/B

Given the function of the form $g(x) = a \cdot e^{x-h} + k$,

  a. Identify *a*, *h*, and *k*.
  b. Identify and plot the reference points.
  c. Draw the graph.
  d. State the domain and range in set notation.

1. $g(x) = 2e^x - 4$

  a. _____

  b. _____

  c.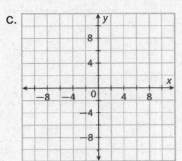

  d. _____

2. $g(x) = e^{x-5} + 3$

  a. _____

  b. _____

  c.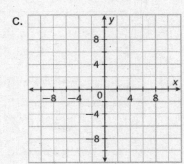

  d. _____

3. $g(x) = 0.5e^{x+4} - 1$

  a. _____

  b. _____

  c.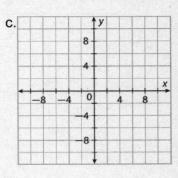

  d. _____

Solve.

4. When interest is compounded continuously, the amount *A* in an account after *t* years is found using the formula $A = Pe^{rt}$, where *P* is the amount of principal and *r* is the annual interest rate.

  a. Use the formula to compute the balance of an investment that had a principal amount of $4500 and earned 5% interest for 6 years.

  _____

  b. What is the amount of interest earned in the investment?

  _____

5. Use the natural decay function, $N(t) = N_0 e^{-kt}$, to find the decay constant, *k*, for a substance that has a half-life of 1000 years.

  _____

LESSON 13-3

The Base e

Practice and Problem Solving: C

Given the function of the form $g(x) = a \cdot e^{x-h} + k,$

   a. Identify *a*, *h*, and *k*.
   b. Identify and plot the reference points.
   c. Draw the graph.
   d. State the domain and range in set notation.

1. $g(x) = \dfrac{1}{5}e^{x-3} - 4$ 2. $g(x) = -4e^{x+2} + 6$ 3. $g(x) = -0.75e^{x-5} + 2.5$

a. _____   a. _____   a. _____

b. _____   b. _____   b. _____

c. 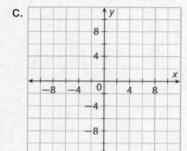   c. 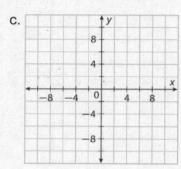   c.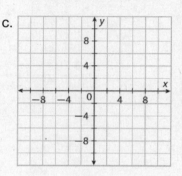

d. _____   d. _____   d. _____

Solve.

4. When interest is compounded continuously, the amount *A* in an account after *t* years is found using the formula $A = Pe^{rt}$, where *P* is the amount of principal and *r* is the annual interest rate. Ariana has a choice of two investments that are both compounded continuously. She can invest $12,000 at 5% for 8 years, or she can invest $9000 at 6.5% for 7 years. Which investment will result in the greater amount of interest earned?

_____

5. Use the natural decay function, $N(t) = N_0 e^{-kt}$, to find the decay rate and the age of a fossil containing 35% of the original amount of a particular substance, given that the substance has a half-life of 2450 years.

_____

LESSON 13-4

Compound Interest

Practice and Problem Solving: A/B

For each investment described, (a) write an exponential growth model that represents the value of the account at any time *t*, and (b) use a graphing calculator to solve for *t* for the given value.

1. The principal amount, $6250, earns 4.25% interest compounded annually. How long will it take for the account's value to surpass $9500?

   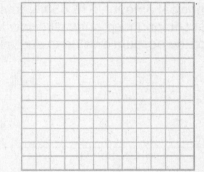

   a. _____

   b. _____

2. The principal amount, $4200, earns 3.6% interest compounded quarterly. How long will it take for the account's value to surpass $15,000?

   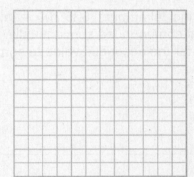

   a. _____

   b. _____

3. The principal amount, $13,000, earns 8.7% interest compounded continuously. How long will it take for the account's value to reach $80,000?

   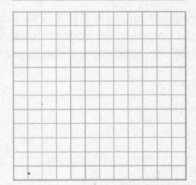

   a. _____

   b. _____

Solve.

4. Shiloh plans to make a deposit into one of the accounts shown in the table. He wants to choose the account with the highest effective interest rate, *R*.

	Account A	Account B
Nominal Interest Rate	4.25%	4.8%
Compounding Period	Monthly	Semiannually

   a. Find R_A and R_B.

   _____

   b. Which account should he choose?

   _____

Compound Interest

LESSON
13-4

Practice and Problem Solving: C

For each investment described, (a) write an exponential growth model that represents the value of the account at any time *t*, and (b) use a graphing calculator to solve for *t* for the given value.

1. The principal amount, $16,550, earns 2.89% interest compounded annually. How long will it take for the account's value to surpass $75,250?

   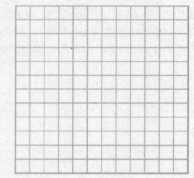

   a. _____

   b. _____

2. The principal amount, $25,700, earns 6.925% interest compounded semiannually. How long will it take for the account's value to surpass $150,000?

   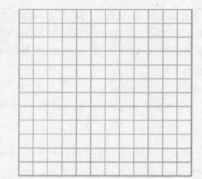

   a. _____

   b. _____

3. The principal amount, $123,500, earns 7.65% interest compounded continuously. How long will it take for the account's value to reach $300,000?

   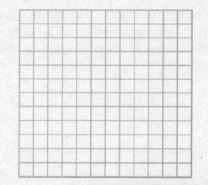

   a. _____

   b. _____

Solve.

4. Yolanda plans to make a deposit into one of the accounts shown in the table. She wants to choose the account with the lowest effective interest rate, *R*.

	Account A	Account B
Nominal Interest Rate	8.25%	8.16%
Compounding Period	Continuously	Monthly

   a. Find R_A and R_B.   _____

   b. Which account should she choose?   _____

LESSON 14-1

Fitting Exponential Functions to Data

Practice and Problem Solving: A/B

Determine whether *f* is an exponential function of *x*. If so, find the constant ratio.

1.

x	−1	0	1	2	3
f(x)	9	3	1	0.3	0.9

_____

2.

x	−1	0	1	2	3
f(x)	0.01	0.03	0.15	0.87	5.19

_____

3.

x	−1	0	1	2	3
f(x)	$\frac{5}{6}$	$\frac{5}{2}$	7.5	22.5	67.5

_____

4.

x	−1	0	1	2	3
f(x)	1	0.5	0.33	0.25	0.2

_____

Use exponential regression to find a function that models the data.

5.

x	1	2	3	4	5
f(x)	14	7.1	3.4	1.8	0.8

_____

6.

x	2	12	22	32	42
f(x)	5	20	80	320	1280

_____

Solve.

7. a. Bernice is selling seashells she has found at the beach. The price of each shell depends on its length. Find an exponential model for the data.

Length of Shell (cm)	5	8	12	20	25
Price ($)	2	3.5	5	18	40

_____

   b. What is the length of a shell selling for $9.00? _____

   c. If Bernice found a 40 cm conch shell, how much could she sell it for? _____

8. a. Use exponential regression to find a function that models this data.

Time (years)	0	10	20	30	40
Population (thousands)	10.1	9.8	17.5	19.9	28.7

_____

   b. When will the population exceed 50 thousand? _____

   c. What will the population be after 100 years? _____

LESSON 14-1
Fitting Exponential Functions to Data
Practice and Problem Solving: C

Determine whether *f* is an exponential function of *x*. If so, find the constant ratio.

1.

x	−1	0	1	2	3
f(x)	3.28	8.4	14.8	22.8	32.8

2.

x	−1	0	1	2	3
f(x)	3.5	7	14	21	28

_____

3.

x	−1	0	1	2	3
f(x)	$\frac{8}{3}$	4	6	9	$\frac{27}{2}$

4.

x	−1	0	1	2	3
f(x)	$\frac{243}{4}$	$\frac{81}{2}$	27	18	12

_____

Use exponential regression to find a function that models the data.

5.

x	1	2	3	4	5
f(x)	9.3	21.8	50.8	118.6	276.6

6.

x	2	4	6	8	10
f(x)	413.2	45.5	4.9	0.6	0.1

_____

7.

x	1	2	3	4	5
f(x)	11.3	8.4	6.3	4.7	3.6

8.

x	2	4	6	8	10
f(x)	14.2	21.3	33.9	57.2	99.8

_____

Solve.

9. a. Use exponential regression to find a function that models this data.

Time (min)	1	3	6	8	10
Bacteria	413	575	945	1316	1832

_____

b. When will the number of bacteria reach 2500? _____

c. How many bacteria will exist after 1 hour? _____

LESSON 14-2

Choosing Among Linear, Quadratic, and Exponential Models

Practice and Problem Solving: A/B

The table below shows the total attendance at major league baseball games, at 10-year intervals since 1930. Use the table for the problems that follow. Round all answers to the nearest thousandth.

Major League Baseball Total Attendance (*y*), in millions, in years since 1930 (*x*)									
x	0	10	20	30	40	50	60	70	80
y	10.1	9.8	17.5	19.9	28.7	43.0	54.8	72.6	73.1

1. Use a graphing calculator to find a linear regression equation for this data.

    _____
    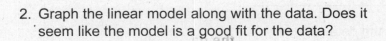

2. Graph the linear model along with the data. Does it seem like the model is a good fit for the data?

    _____
    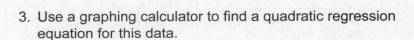

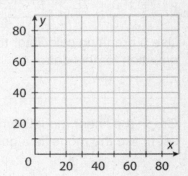

3. Use a graphing calculator to find a quadratic regression equation for this data.

    _____
    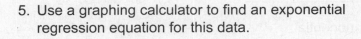

4. Graph the quadratic model along with the data. Does it seem like the model is a good fit for the data?

    _____
    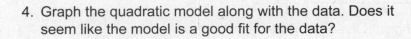

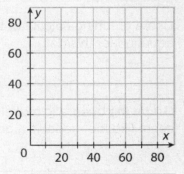

5. Use a graphing calculator to find an exponential regression equation for this data.

    _____
    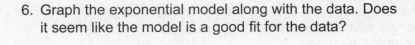

6. Graph the exponential model along with the data. Does it seem like the model is a good fit for the data?

    _____

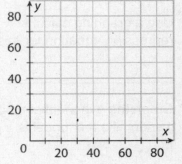

7. Use the exponential regression equation to predict major league baseball attendance in 2020. Based on the pattern of data, do you think this is a reasonable prediction? Explain.

    _____

LESSON 14-2

Choosing Among Linear, Quadratic, and Exponential Models

Practice and Problem Solving: C

A pot of boiling water is allowed to cool for 50 minutes. The table below shows the temperature of the water as it cools. Use the table for the problems that follow. Round all answers to the nearest thousandth.

Temperature of Water (y), in degrees Celsius, after cooling for x minutes											
x	0	5	10	15	20	25	30	35	40	45	50
y	100	75	57	44	34	26	21	17	14	11	10

1. Use a graphing calculator to find a linear regression equation for this data.

   _____

2. Graph the linear model along with the data. Does it seem like the model is a good fit for the data?

   _____

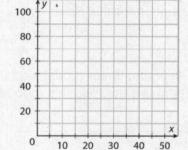

3. Use a graphing calculator to find a quadratic regression equation for this data.

   _____

4. Graph the quadratic model along with the data. Does it seem like the model is a good fit for the data?

   _____

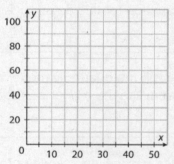

5. Use a graphing calculator to find an exponential regression equation for this data.

   _____

6. Graph the exponential model along with the data. Does it seem like the model is a good fit for the data?

   _____

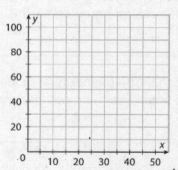

7. Use each regression model to estimate the temperature of the water after 55 minutes. Which estimation seems the most likely?

   _____

Name _____ Date _____ Class_____

Defining and Evaluating a Logarithmic Function
Practice and Problem Solving: A/B

Write each exponential equation in logarithmic form.

1. $3^7 = 2187$

2. $12^2 = 144$

3. $5^3 = 125$

_____   _____   _____

Write each logarithmic equation in exponential form.

4. $\log_{10} 100{,}000 = 5$

5. $\log_4 1024 = 5$

6. $\log_9 729 = 3$

_____   _____   _____

Evaluate each expression without using a calculator.

7. $\log 1{,}000{,}000$

8. $\log 10$

9. $\log 1$

_____   _____   _____

10. $\log_4 16$

11. $\log_8 1$

12. $\log_5 625$

_____   _____   _____

Use the given *x*-values to graph each function. Then graph its inverse. Write an equation for the inverse function and describe its domain and range.

13. $f(x) = 2^x$; $x = -2, -1, 0, 1, 2, 3, 4$

14. $f(x) = \left(\dfrac{1}{2}\right)^x$; $x = -3, -2, -1, 0, 1, 2, 3$

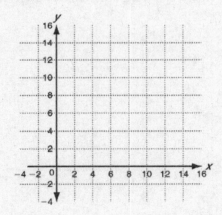

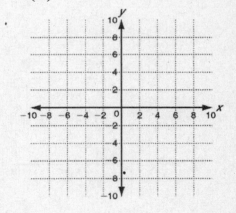

_____   _____

Solve.

15. The acidity level, or pH, of a liquid is given by the formula $pH = \log \dfrac{1}{[H^+]}$, where $[H^+]$ is the concentration (in moles per liter) of hydrogen ions in the liquid. The hydrogen ion concentration in moles per liter for a certain brand of tomato vegetable juice is 0.000316.

   a. Write a logarithmic equation for the pH of the juice.   _____

   b. What is the pH of the juice?   _____

LESSON 15-1
Defining and Evaluating a Logarithmic Function
Practice and Problem Solving: C

Write each exponential equation in logarithmic form.

1. $20^3 = 8000$

2. $11^4 = 14{,}641$

3. $a^b = c$

_____ _____ _____

Write each logarithmic equation in exponential form.

4. $\log_{10} 10{,}000{,}000 = 7$

5. $\log_6 216 = 3$

6. $\log_p q = r$

_____ _____ _____

Evaluate each expression without using a calculator.

7. $\log 1$

8. $\log 10{,}000$

9. $\log 1000$

_____ _____ _____

10. $\log_5 3125$

11. $\log_{15} 1$

12. $\log_4 256$

_____ _____ _____

Use the given *x*-values to graph each function. Then graph its inverse. Write an equation for the inverse function and describe its domain and range.

13. $f(x) = 0.1^x$; $x = -1, 0, 1, 2$

14. $f(x) = \left(\dfrac{5}{2}\right)^x$; $x = -3, -2, -1, 0, 1, 2, 3$

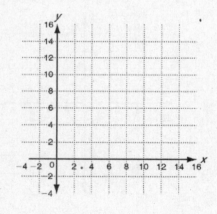 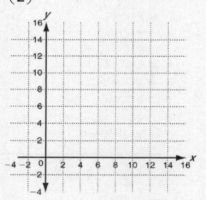

_____ _____

Solve.

15. The acidity level, or pH, of a liquid is given by the formula $\mathrm{pH} = \log \dfrac{1}{[\mathrm{H}^+]}$, where $[\mathrm{H}^+]$ is the concentration (in moles per liter) of hydrogen ions in the liquid. The hydrogen ion concentration in moles per liter of a certain solvent is 0.00794.

a. Write a logarithmic equation for the pH of the solvent. _____

b. What is the pH of the solvent? _____

**LESSON
15-2**

Graphing Logarithmic Functions

Practice and Problem Solving: A/B

Graph each function. Find the asymptote. Tell how the graph is transformed from the graph of its parent function.

1. $f(x) = \log_2 x + 4$

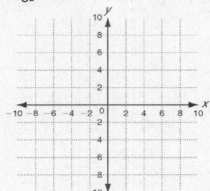

_____

2. $f(x) = 3\log_4 (x + 6)$

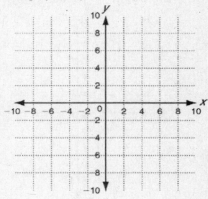

_____

3. $f(x) = \log (x + 5)$

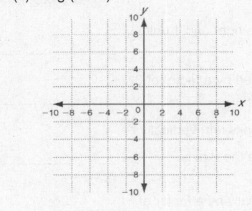

_____

4. $f(x) = 3 + \ln x$

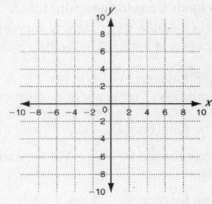

_____

Write each transformed function.

5. The function $f(x) = \log (x + 1)$ is reflected across the *x*-axis and translated down 4 units.

_____

6. The function $f(x) = \log_8 (x - 3)$ is compressed vertically by a factor of $\frac{2}{5}$

and translated up 11 units.

_____

Solve.

7. The function $A(t) = Pe^{rt}$ is used to calculate the balance, *A*, of an investment in which the interest is compounded continuously at an annual rate, *r*, over *t* years. Find the inverse of the formula. Describe what information the inverse gives.

LESSON 15-2

Graphing Logarithmic Functions

Practice and Problem Solving: C

Graph each function. Find the asymptote. Tell how the graph is transformed from the graph of the parent function.

1. $f(x) = 2.5\log_2(x + 7) - 3$

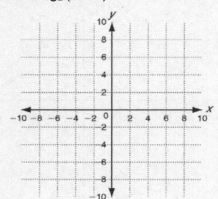

_____

2. $f(x) = -0.8\ln(x - 1.5) + 2$

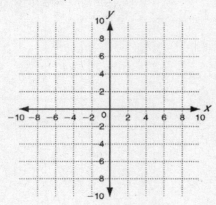

_____

Write each transformed function.

3. The function $f(x) = -\log_9(x + 4)$ is translated 4 units right and 1 unit down and vertically stretched by a factor of 7.

_____

4. The function $f(x) = 3\ln(2x + 8)$ is vertically stretched by a factor of 3, translated 7 units up, and reflected across the *x*-axis.

_____

5. The function $f(x) = -\log(5 - x) - 2$ is translated 6 units left, vertically compressed by a factor of $\frac{1}{3}$, and reflected across the *x*-axis.

_____

6. The function $f(x) = 8\log_7 x - 5$ is compressed vertically by a factor of 0.5, translated right 1 unit, and reflected across the *x*-axis.

_____

7. What transformations does the function $f(x) = -\ln(x + 1) - 2$ undergo to become the function $g(x) = \ln(x - 1)$?

_____

Solve.

8. The function $A(t) = Pe^{rt}$ is used to calculate the balance, *A*, of an investment where the interest is compounded continuously at an annual rate, *r*, over *t* years. Find the inverse of the formula. Then use it to determine the amount of time it will take a $27,650 investment at 3.95% to reach a balance of $50,000.

_____

LESSON 16-1

Properties of Logarithms

Practice and Problem Solving: A/B

Express as a single logarithm. Simplify, if possible.

1. $\log_3 9 + \log_3 27$

_____

2. $\log_2 8 + \log_2 16$

_____

3. $\log_{10} 80 + \log_{10} 125$

_____

4. $\log_6 8 + \log_6 27$

_____

5. $\log_3 6 + \log_3 13.5$

_____

6. $\log_4 32 + \log_4 128$

_____

Express as a single logarithm. Simplify, if possible.

7. $\log_2 80 - \log_2 10$

_____

8. $\log_{10} 4000 - \log_{10} 40$

_____

9. $\log_4 384 - \log_4 6$

_____

10. $\log_2 1920 - \log_2 30$

_____

11. $\log_3 486 - \log_3 2$

_____

12. $\log_6 180 - \log_6 5$

_____

Simplify, if possible.

13. $\log_4 4^6$

_____

14. $\log_5 5^{x-5}$

_____

15. $7^{\log_7 30}$

_____

16. $12^{\log_{12} 1}$

_____

17. $\log_8 8^5$

_____

18. $\log_3 9^4$

_____

Evaluate. Round to the nearest hundredth.

19. $\log_{12} 1$

_____

20. $\log_3 30$

_____

21. $\log_5 10$

_____

Solve.

22. The Richter magnitude of an earthquake, *M*, is related to the energy released in ergs, *E*, by the formula $M = \dfrac{2}{3}\log\left(\dfrac{E}{10^{11.8}}\right)$.

Find the energy released by an earthquake of magnitude 4.2. _____

LESSON 16-1 Properties of Logarithms

Practice and Problem Solving: C

Express as a single logarithm. Simplify, if possible.

1. $\log_6 12 + \log_6 18$

2. $\log_3 81 - \log_3 27$

3. $\log_4 128 - \log_4 8$

_____

_____

_____

4. $\log_6 18 + \log_6 72$

5. $\log_5 3125 - \log_5 25$

6. $\log_8 128 + \log_8 256$

_____

_____

_____

7. $\log_5 5 + \log_5 125$

8. $\log_2 256 - \log_2 64$

9. $\log_3 8019 - \log_3 99$

_____

_____

_____

10. $\log_8 80 + \log_8 51.2$

11. $\log_7 13.3 - \log_7 1.9$

12. $\log_{10} 125 + \log_{10} 80$

_____

_____

_____

Evaluate. Round to the nearest hundredth.

13. $\log_8 8^6$

14. $2^{\log_2 8^x}$

15. $\log_2 16^5$

_____

_____

_____

16. $\log_3 3^{(2x + 1)}$

17. $\log_4 16^{(x - 1)}$

18. $5^{\log_5 17}$

_____

_____

_____

19. $\log_3 5^2$

20. $\log_5 \left(\dfrac{1}{125}\right)^2$

21. $\log_6 \left(\dfrac{1}{6^4}\right)^3$

_____

_____

_____

22. $\log_4 20^2$

23. $\log_9 27^4$

24. $\log_2 10$

_____

_____

_____

Solve.

25. Carmen has a painting presently valued at $5000. An art dealer told her the painting would appreciate at a rate of 6% per year. In how many years will the painting be worth $8000?

a. Write a logarithmic expression representing the situation. _____

b. Simplify your expression. How many years will it take? _____

LESSON 16-2

Solving Exponential Equations

Practice and Problem Solving: A/B

Solve each equation by graphing. If necessary, round to the nearest thousandth.

1. $5e^{x-3} = 75$

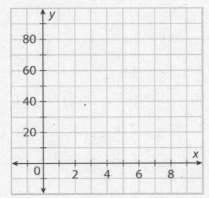

2. $8e^{-8x} + 8 = 17$

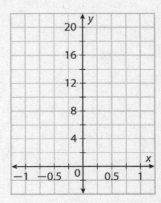

_____   _____

Solve each equation algebraically. If necessary, round to the nearest thousandth.

3. $5^{2x} = 20$

4. $12^{2x-8} = 15$

5. $2^{x+6} = 4$

_____   _____   _____

6. $16^{5x} = 64^{x+7}$

7. $243^{0.2x} = 81^{x+5}$

8. $25^x = 125^{x-2}$

_____   _____   _____

9. $\left(\dfrac{1}{2}\right)^x = 16^2$

10. $\left(\dfrac{1}{32}\right)^{2x} = 64$

11. $\left(\dfrac{1}{27}\right)^{x-6} = 27$

_____   _____   _____

12. $6e^{10x-8} - 4 = 34$

13. $8(10)^{7x-6} - 8 = 59$

14. $-6e^{-4x-1} + 3 = -37$

_____   _____   _____

Solve.

15. The population of a small farming community is declining at a rate of 7% per year. The decline can be expressed by the exponential equation $P = C(1 - 0.07)^t$, where P is the population after t years and C is the current population. If the population was 8500 in 2004, when will the population be less than 6000?

_____

LESSON
16-2

Solving Exponential Equations

Practice and Problem Solving: C

Solve each equation by graphing. If necessary, round to the nearest thousandth.

1. $e^{0.5x-9} + 0.2 = 73$

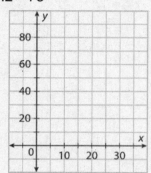

2. $9e^{x-7} - 5.5 = 51$

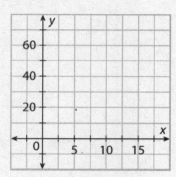

_____   _____

Solve each equation algebraically. If necessary, round to the nearest thousandth.

3. $16^{3x} = 8^{x+6}$

_____

4. $3e^{2x-3} - 4 = 78$

_____

5. $12^{x-1} = 20^2$

_____

6. $9^{2x} = 27^{x+4}$

_____

7. $256^{0.5x} = 64^{2x+5}$

_____

8. $216^{\frac{x}{3}} = 36^{2x+3}$

_____

9. $\left(\dfrac{1}{9}\right)^{3x} = 27$

_____

10. $\left(\dfrac{1}{16}\right)^{x+5} = 8^2$

_____

11. $\left(\dfrac{2}{5}\right)^{8x} = \left(\dfrac{25}{4}\right)^2$

_____

12. $-7(10)^{8-10x} + 9 = 4$

_____

13. $-3(10)^{4-x} - 4 = -91$

_____

14. $10e^{8x+1} - 3 = 70$

_____

Solve.

15. Lorena deposited $9000 into an account that earns 4.25% interest each year.

    a. Write an equation for the amount, *A*, in the account after *t* years.

        _____

    b. In how many years will her account exceed $20,000?

        _____

    c. If she waits for 50 years, how much will be in her account?

        _____

Name _____ Date _____ Class_____

LESSON 17-1

Angles of Rotation and Radian Measure

Practice and Problem Solving: A/B

Draw an angle with the given measure in standard position.

1. −420°

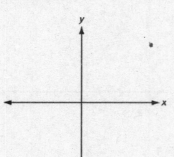

2. 405°

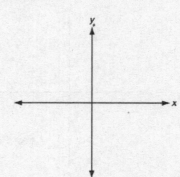

3. −450°

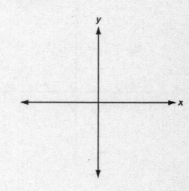

Find the measures of a positive angle and a negative angle that are coterminal with each given angle.

4. $\theta = 425°$

_____

5. $\theta = -316°$

_____

6. $\theta = -800°$

_____

7. $\theta = 281°$

_____

8. $\theta = -4°$

_____

9. $\theta = 743°$

_____

Convert each measure from degrees to radians or from radians to degrees.

10. $\dfrac{5\pi}{12}$

_____

11. 215°

_____

12. $-\dfrac{29\pi}{18}$

_____

13. −180°

_____

14. $\dfrac{5\pi}{3}$

_____

15. $-\dfrac{7\pi}{6}$

_____

Solve.

16. San Antonio, Texas, is located about 30° north of the equator. If Earth's radius is about 3959 miles, approximately how many miles is San Antonio from the equator?

_____

LESSON 17-1

Angles of Rotation and Radian Measure

Practice and Problem Solving: C

Draw an angle with the given measure in standard position.

1. 550°

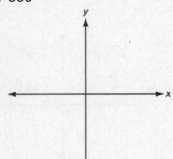

2. −645°

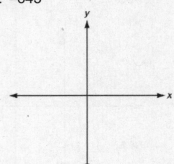

3. 715°

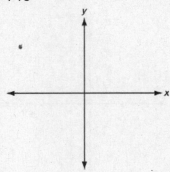

Find the measures of a positive angle and a negative angle that are coterminal with each given angle.

4. $\theta = 400°$

_____

5. $\theta = -360°$

_____

6. $\theta = -1010°$

_____

7. $\theta = 567°$

_____

8. $\theta = -164°$

_____

9. $\theta = 358°$

_____

Convert each measure from degrees to radians or from radians to degrees.

10. $-\dfrac{3\pi}{2}$

_____

11. 450°

_____

12. $\dfrac{5\pi}{18}$

_____

13. −200°

_____

14. $\dfrac{7\pi}{4}$

_____

15. $-\dfrac{11\pi}{6}$

_____

Solve.

16. A pendulum is 18 feet long. Its central angle is 44°. The pendulum makes one back and forth swing every 12 seconds. To the nearest foot, how far does the pendulum swing each minute?

_____

LESSON 17-2

Defining and Evaluating the Basic Trigonometric Functions

Practice and Problem Solving: A/B

Find the measure of the reference angle for each given angle.

1. $\theta = 220°$

2. $\theta = \dfrac{11\pi}{6}$

3. $\theta = -235°$

_____

_____

_____

4. $\theta = -\dfrac{2\pi}{3}$

5. $\theta = 590°$

6. $\theta = -\dfrac{13\pi}{4}$

_____

_____

_____

Find the exact value of each trigonometric function.

7. $\cos 120°$

8. $\sin \dfrac{4\pi}{3}$

9. $\sin 585°$

_____

_____

_____

10. $\tan 765°$

11. $\cos \dfrac{9\pi}{2}$

12. $\tan -\dfrac{5\pi}{6}$

_____

_____

_____

Use a calculator to evaluate each trigonometric function. Round to four decimal places.

13. $\sin 170°$

14. $\tan \dfrac{7\pi}{9}$

15. $\sin -\dfrac{8\pi}{3}$

_____

_____

_____

16. $\cos -71°$

17. $\tan 25°$

18. $\cos -\dfrac{21\pi}{5}$

_____

_____

_____

Solve. Assume each circle is centered at 0.

19. Find the exact coordinates of the point on a circle of radius 12.5 at an angle of 180°.

_____

20. Find the exact coordinates of the point on a circle of radius 7 at an angle of $\dfrac{5\pi}{4}$.

_____

LESSON 17-2

Defining and Evaluating the Basic Trigonometric Functions

Practice and Problem Solving: C

Find the measure of the reference angle for each given angle.

1. $\theta = 580°$

2. $\theta = -\dfrac{15\pi}{4}$

3. $\theta = -375°$

_____ _____ _____

4. $\theta = \dfrac{67\pi}{18}$

5. $\theta = -705°$

6. $\theta = -\dfrac{22\pi}{9}$

_____ _____ _____

Find the exact value of each trigonometric function.

7. $\cos 870°$

8. $\sin -\dfrac{19\pi}{6}$

9. $\sin -240°$

_____ _____ _____

10. $\tan -945°$

11. $\cos \dfrac{23\pi}{4}$

12. $\tan \dfrac{13\pi}{6}$

_____ _____ _____

Use a calculator to evaluate each trigonometric function. Round to four decimal places.

13. $\sin -840°$

14. $\tan \dfrac{19\pi}{18}$

15. $\sin \dfrac{341\pi}{60}$

_____ _____ _____

16. $\cos -760°$

17. $\tan -634°$

18. $\cos \dfrac{47\pi}{36}$

_____ _____ _____

Solve. Assume each circle is centered at 0.

19. Find the exact coordinates of the point on a circle of radius 7.25 at an angle of 315°.

_____

20. Find the exact coordinates of the point on a circle of radius 5 at an angle of $\dfrac{5\pi}{3}$.

_____

LESSON
17-3

Using a Pythagorean Identity

Practice and Problem Solving: A/B

Use the given value to calculate the values of the indicated trigonometric functions. Round your answers to three decimal places.

1. Given that $\cos \theta \approx 0.707$, where $0 < \theta < \dfrac{\pi}{2}$, find $\sin \theta$.

_____

2. Given that $\sin \theta \approx -0.866$, where $\pi < \theta < \dfrac{3\pi}{2}$, find $\cos \theta$.

_____

3. Given that $\tan \theta \approx 1.072$, where $0 < \theta < \dfrac{\pi}{2}$, find the values of $\sin \theta$ and $\cos \theta$.

_____

4. Given that $\cos \theta \approx -0.485$, where $\dfrac{\pi}{2} < \theta < \pi$, find $\sin \theta$.

_____

5. Given that $\tan \theta \approx -0.087$, where $\dfrac{3\pi}{2} < \theta < 2\pi$, find the values of $\sin \theta$ and $\cos \theta$.

_____

6. Given that $\sin \theta = 0.5$, where $\dfrac{\pi}{2} < \theta < \pi$, find $\cos \theta$.

_____

7. Given that $\sin \theta \approx -0.829$, where $\pi < \theta < \dfrac{3\pi}{2}$, find $\cos \theta$.

_____

Solve.

8. The instant at which a waxed wood block on an inclined plane of wet snow begins to slide is represented by the equation $mg \sin \theta = \mu mg \cos \theta$, where θ represents the angle of the plane and μ is the coefficient of friction. What is $\cos \theta$ if $\mu = 0.52$ and $\sin \theta \approx 0.461$?

_____

LESSON
17-3

Using a Pythagorean Identity
Practice and Problem Solving: C

Use the given value to calculate the values of the indicated trigonometric functions. Round your answers to three decimal places.

1. Given that sin $\theta \approx 0.899$, where $0 < \theta < \dfrac{\pi}{2}$, find cos θ.

   _____

2. Given that cos $\theta \approx -0.342$, where $\pi < \theta < \dfrac{3\pi}{2}$, find sin θ.

   _____

3. Given that tan $\theta \approx 1.376$, where $0 < \theta < \dfrac{\pi}{2}$, find the values of sin θ and cos θ.

   _____

4. Given that sin $\theta \approx 0.839$, where $\dfrac{\pi}{2} < \theta < \pi$, find cos θ.

   _____

5. Given that tan $\theta \approx -0.384$, where $\dfrac{3\pi}{2} < \theta < 2\pi$, find the values of sin θ and cos θ.

   _____

6. Given that cos $\theta \approx -0.438$, where $\dfrac{\pi}{2} < \theta < \pi$, find sin θ.

   _____

7. Given that cos $\theta \approx -0.326$, where $\pi < \theta < \dfrac{3\pi}{2}$, find sin θ.

   _____

Solve.

8. Alan is using the equation $mg \sin \theta = \mu mg \cos \theta$ to determine the coefficient of friction, μ, between a flat rock and a metal ramp, where θ represents the angle of the ramp. Find μ to the nearest hundredth if sin $\theta \approx 0.321$.

   _____

LESSON
18-1

Stretching, Compressing, and Reflecting Sine and Cosine Graphs
Practice and Problem Solving: A/B

Using $f(x) = \sin x$ or $g(x) = \cos x$ as a guide, graph each function. Identify the amplitude and period.

1. $b(x) = -5\sin \pi x$

_____

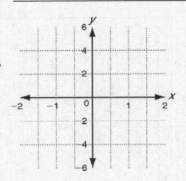

2. $k(x) = 3\cos 2\pi x$

_____

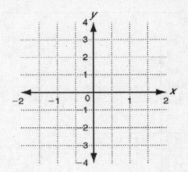

Using $f(x) = \sin x$ or $g(x) = \cos x$ as a guide, graph each function. Identify the period and asymptotes.

3. $k(x) = \sec \dfrac{x}{2}$

_____

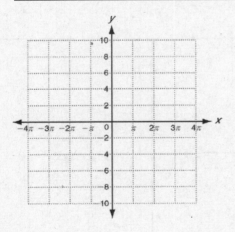

4. $q(x) = \dfrac{1}{2}\csc(2x)$

_____

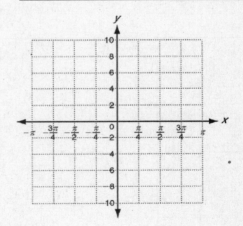

Solve.

5. a. Use a sine function to graph a sound wave with a period of 0.002 second and an amplitude of 2 centimeters.

   b. Find the frequency in hertz for this sound wave.

_____

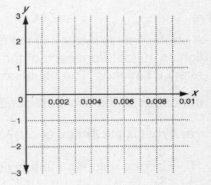

Name _____ Date _____ Class_____

LESSON 18-1

Stretching, Compressing, and Reflecting Sine and Cosine Graphs
Practice and Problem Solving: C

Using $f(x) = \sin x$ or $f(x) = \cos x$ as a guide, graph each function. Identify the amplitude, period, and x-intercepts.

1. $h(x) = \dfrac{1}{2}\cos(-\pi x)$

2. $q(x) = -\sin\left(\dfrac{\pi}{2}x\right)$

_____

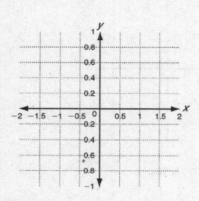

_____

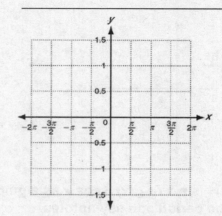

Using $f(x) = \cos x$ or $f(x) = \sin x$ as a guide, graph each function. Identify the period and asymptotes.

3. $k(x) = \sec\dfrac{x}{4}$

4. $q(x) = 2\csc(2x)$

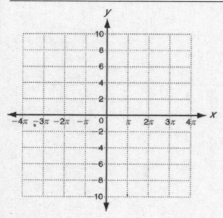

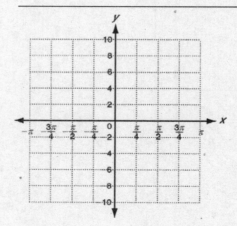

Solve.

5. A strobe light is located in the center of a square dance room. The rotating light is 40 feet from each of the 4 walls and completes one full rotation every 6 seconds. The equation representing the distance d in feet that

   the center of the circle of light is from the light source is $d(t) = 40\sec\left(\dfrac{\pi t}{3}\right)$.

   a. What is the period of $d(t)$? _____

   b. Find the value of the function at $t = 2.5$. _____

LESSON 18-2

Stretching, Compressing, and Reflecting Tangent Graphs
Practice and Problem Solving: A/B

Write the function rule for the transformed tangent function shown.

Use the form $f(x) = a\tan\left(\dfrac{x}{b}\right)$.

1.

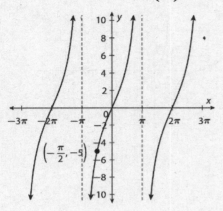

_____

2.

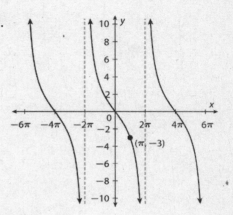

_____

For each rule given for a transformed tangent function, find the asymptotes and reference points for one cycle. Then graph the function.

3. $f(x) = \dfrac{1}{2}\tan(3x)$

Asymptotes: _____

Reference Points: _____

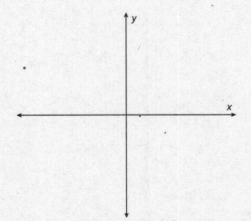

4. $f(x) = -4\tan\left(\dfrac{x}{5}\right)$

Asymptotes: _____

Reference Points: _____

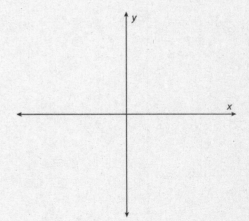

LESSON
18-2

Stretching, Compressing, and Reflecting Tangent Graphs
Practice and Problem Solving: C

Write the function rule for the transformed tangent function shown.

Use the form $f(x) = a\tan\left(\dfrac{x}{b}\right)$.

1.

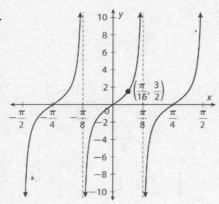

_____

2.

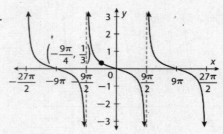

_____

For each rule given for a transformed tangent function, find the asymptotes and reference points for one cycle. Then graph the function.

3. $f(x) = -\dfrac{5}{4}\tan\left(\dfrac{x}{3}\right)$

   Asymptotes: _____

   Reference Points: _____

4. $f(x) = 2.2\tan(0.25x)$

   Asymptotes: _____

   Reference Points: _____

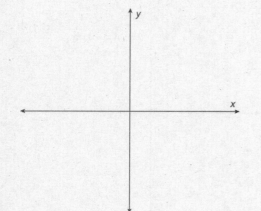

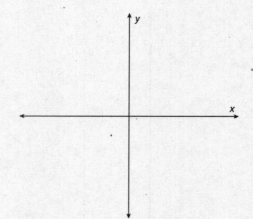

LESSON 18-3

Translating Trigonometric Graphs

Practice and Problem Solving: A/B

For each rule given, identify the indicated points for one cycle. Then graph the function.

1. $f(x) = 2\sin\frac{1}{4}(x - 3\pi)$

Starting point: _____

Ending point: _____

Middle point: _____

Local minimum: _____

Local maximum: _____

2. $f(x) = \frac{1}{2}\cos\frac{1}{4}\left(x - \frac{\pi}{2}\right) + 1$

Starting point: _____

Ending point: _____

Middle point: _____

1st Midline point: _____

2nd midline point: _____

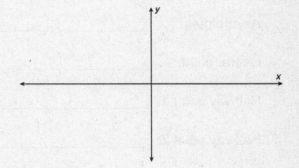

Write a function rule for the indicated trigonometric function.

3. Write a tangent function for the graph. (Hint: Use the key points and asymptotes shown on the graph.)

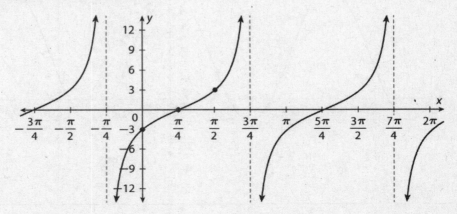

LESSON 18-3

Translating Trigonometric Graphs

Practice and Problem Solving: C

For each rule given, identify the indicated points or features for one cycle. Then graph the function.

1. $f(x) = \dfrac{3}{4}\cos 2\left(x + \dfrac{\pi}{3}\right) - 3$

Starting point: _____

Ending point: _____

Middle point: _____

1st Midline point: _____

2nd midline point: _____

2. $f(x) = \dfrac{2}{5}\tan 3(x - \pi) + 4$

Asymptotes: _____

Center point: _____

Halfway point 1: _____

Halfway point 2: _____

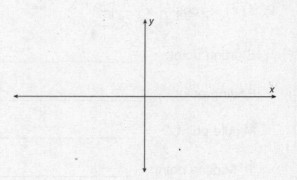

Write a function rule for the indicated trigonometric function.

3. Write a sine function for the graph.

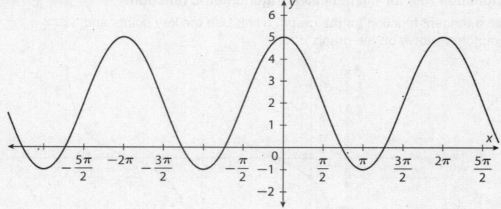

_____

Fitting Sine Functions to Data

LESSON 18-4

Practice and Problem Solving: A/B

The data in the table represents the average daily temperatures *T*, in degrees Fahrenheit, for a city over a 12 month period. Use the data for Problems 1–5. Round to two decimal places when necessary.

Month	1	2	3	4	5	6	7	8	9	10	11	12
$T(°F)$	−7.8	−1.3	13.3	33	50.9	62.1	64.8	59.1	47.8	27.4	5	−4.2

1. Estimate the amplitude *A*, the period *P*, the phase shift *h*, and equation of the midline *k*(*x*) for a sine function that models this data.

   _____

2. Use the factors to write a sine function that models the data.

   _____

3. Use the SinReg function on a graphing calculator to obtain a sine regression model for the data.

   _____

4. Rewrite the regression equation and compare it to the model you created using the factors.

   _____

5. Graph both models, along with the data points, on your graphing calculator. Sketch the result below.

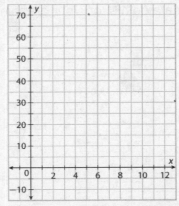

6. Use the intersect feature on your graphing calculator to find the intersection points of both models with the line *y* = 10. Compare and interpret the results.

   _____

   _____

Fitting Sine Functions to Data

LESSON 18-4

Practice and Problem Solving: C

The data in the table represents the height, in meters, of a pendulum as it swings over time, in seconds. Use the data for Problems 1–6. Round to three decimal places when necessary.

Time (sec)	0.12	0.24	0.36	0.42	0.48	0.6	0.72
Height (m)	0.663	1.167	0.995	0.864	0.655	1.215	0.929

0.84	0.96	1.08	1.14	1.2	1.32	1.44
0.659	1.254	0.865	0.755	0.676	1.281	0.807

1. Estimate the amplitude A, the period P, the phase shift h, and equation of the midline $k(x)$ for a sine function that models this data.

   _____

2. Use the factors to write a sine function that models the data.

   _____

3. Use the SinReg function on a graphing calculator to obtain a sine regression model for the data.

   _____

4. Rewrite the regression equation and compare it to the model you created using the factors.

   _____

5. Graph both models, along with the data points, on your graphing calculator. Sketch the result below.

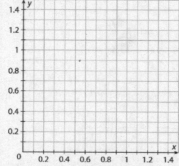

6. For each model, find the first two times the pendulum reaches a height of 1.2 meters. Compare your result to the graphs of the models. How do you think the results would differ as time increases?

   _____

   _____

LESSON 19-1

Probability and Set Theory

Practice and Problem Solving: A/B

For Problems 1–6, write each statement in set notation. Use the descriptions of the sets to the right to complete each statement.

1. the intersection of sets *A* and *B*

   _____

2. the complement of set *A*

   _____

$A = \{21, 23, 25, 27, 29\}$
$B = \{21, 24, 27, 30\}$
$U = \{20, 21, 22, 23, 24, 25, 26,$ $27, 28, 29, 30\}$

3. the union of sets *A* and *B* _____

4. the complement of set *B* _____

5. the number of elements in set *A* _____

6. the number of elements in set *B* _____

7. Define set *C* so that *C* is a subset of set *A*. _____

8. Define set *D* so that *D* is a subset of set *B*. _____

For Problems 9 and 10, use the descriptions of the sets in the box above.

9. Create a Venn diagram to represent sets *A, B,* and *U*.

10. Describe the parts of the Venn diagram that correspond to 1–4 above.

    1) _____

    2) _____

    3) _____

    4) _____

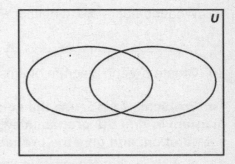

Refer to the descriptions of the sets above and the Venn diagram to find the probabilities in Problems 11–14.

11. Use set notation to write a fraction giving the probability that a number chosen from the universal set will be in set *A*. Fill in the numbers.

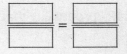

12. What is the probability that a number in *U* is *not* in *A*? _____

13. What is the probability that a number in *U* is in $A \cup B$? _____

14. What is the probability that a number in *U* is *not* in *A* or *B*? _____

LESSON
19-1

Probability and Set Theory

Practice and Problem Solving: C

For Problems 1–7, the universal set consists of the natural numbers from 1 to 20. For each description, write a statement in set notation.

1. Set *P* _____

2. Set *T* _____

3. Set *F* _____

Set *U*: integers from 1 to 20
Set *P*: prime numbers
Set *T*: multiples of 3
Set *F*: multiples of 5

4. number of elements in set *P* _____

5. intersection of sets *P* and *T* _____

6. union of sets *T* and *F* _____

7. complement of set *P* _____

Use the sets above to solve Problems 8–10.

8. Explain why the intersection of all three sets, *P, T,* and *F,* is the empty set.

_____

_____

9. What numbers are in neither *P, T,* nor *F*?

_____

10. Create a Venn diagram of these sets.

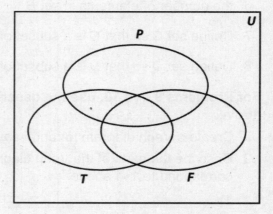

For Problems 11–15, use the sets defined above and your Venn diagram to find the probabilities. Write each probability statement in set notation, and give the probabilities in simplest form.

11. probability that a number in the universal set is a multiple of 3

_____

12. probability that a number in the universal set is *not* a multiple of 3

_____

13. What is $P(T) + P(\sim T)$? _____

14. probability that a number in the universal set is a multiple of *both* 3 and 5

_____

15. probability that a number in the universal set is prime or a multiple of 5

_____

LESSON
19-2

Permutations and Probability

Practice and Problem Solving: A/B

For Problems 1–8, give the value of each expression.

1. 5! = _____

2. 6! = _____

3. 7! = _____

4. $\dfrac{6!}{5!}$ = _____

5. $\dfrac{7!}{6!}$ = _____

6. $\dfrac{8!}{7!}$ = _____

7. Suppose n stands for any number. Write a fraction to show n factorial

   divided by $(n-1)$ factorial. Find its value. _____

8. What is the value of $\dfrac{n!}{(n-2)!}$? _____

Use the Fundamental Counting Principle to solve Problems 9–11.

9. Alicia is designing a flag with 3 stripes. She has 5 different colors of fabric to use in any order she likes, but she does not want 2 stripes next to each other to be the same color. How many different color patterns can she choose from? Explain your answer. _____

10. A travel agent is offering a vacation package. Participants choose the type of tour, a meal plan, and a hotel class from the chart to the right. How many different vacation packages

    are offered? _____

Tour	Meal	Hotel
Walking	Restaurant	4-Star
Boat	Picnic	3-Star
Bicycle		2-Star
		1-Star

11. There are 8 marbles in a bag, all of different colors. In how many orders can 4 marbles be chosen? _____

For Problems 12–14, find the probabilities.

12. Gil's padlock can be opened by entering 3 digits in the right order (digits can be repeated). How many different orders of digits are there? What is the probability that someone could guess the right order on the first try?

    _____

    _____

13. A playlist includes 8 songs, including Kim's favorite and second favorite. How many different ways can the playlist be shuffled? What is the probability that Kim's favorite song will be first and her second favorite song will be second? Explain your answers.

    _____

    _____

    _____

14. What is the probability that a family with 4 children will have all girls? _____

Permutations and Probability

LESSON 19-2

Practice and Problem Solving: C

For Problems 1–4, evaluate each expression.

1. $\dfrac{7! - 4!}{(6-3)!} =$ _____

2. $\dfrac{6!}{3!(8-5)!} =$ _____

3. $\dfrac{5!\,4!}{9!} =$ _____

4. $\dfrac{11!}{6!\,5!} =$ _____

For Problems 5–9, find the number of permutations.

5. A 10-person board of trustees is choosing a chairperson, a secretary, and a publicist. If they have already decided upon a chairperson, in how many ways can they choose a secretary and a publicist? _____

6. The door code to gain access to a top-secret laboratory is 6 digits. The first 3 digits of the code are all odd, and the last 3 digits are all even. Digits can be used more than once. How many possible codes are there?

7. Find the number of different permutations of the letters in the word INVISIBILITY. _____

8. How many ways can the letters from *A* through *H* be used to create 5-letter passwords if there are no repeated letters? _____

9. The 13 diamonds from a deck of cards are shuffled and laid out in a row. How many arrangements are possible if the first card is the ace? If the first card is a face card (J, Q, K)? Explain your answers. _____

_____

For Problems 10–12, find the probabilities.

10. Miguel is trying to remember Aerin's phone number. He knows that the last 4 digits include a 3, a 7, and two 6s, but he's not sure about the order. What is the probability that he will guess correctly? _____

11. Fran needs to create an 8-character password with any combination of digits and/or letters. What is the probability that her password will be identical to someone else's? (Write your answer in exponential form.) _____

12. Charlene and Amir are scrambling the letters in words to play a word game. What is the probability that they will scramble the word LANGUAGE the same way? _____

LESSON 19-3

Combinations and Probability

Practice and Problem Solving: A/B

Use the scenario in the box for Problems 1–4.

1. Explain why you should use combinations rather than permutations for this problem.

   _____

> Calvin has enough money to get 3 new T-shirts at a buy two, get one free sale. There are 8 color choices, and he wants to get 3 different colors. How many possible combinations of 3 colors are there?

2. Tell what the variables n and r stand for in the
   combinations formula, $_nC_r = \dfrac{n!}{r!(n-r)!}$, and identify
   their values for this problem.

   n _____ r _____

3. Substitute the values of n and r into the formula and solve to find the number of combinations of 3 T-shirts. _____

4. The formula for combinations is equal to the formula for permutations divided by $r!$ Explain how dividing by $r!$ relates to this problem.

   _____

   _____

5. Find the number of combinations of 7 objects taken 4 at a time. _____

6. Rachel has 10 valuable baseball cards. She wants to select 2 of them to sell online. How many different combinations of 2 cards could she choose? _____

7. If Rachel picked the cards at random, what is the probability that one of the 2 cards would be her Ken Griffey, Jr., card? Explain your answer. _____

   _____

8. Mrs. Marshall has 11 boys and 14 girls in her kindergarten class. In how many ways can she select 2 boys to pass out a snack? _____

9. In how many ways can Mrs. Marshall select 3 students to carry papers to the office? Show your calculations. _____

10. What is the probability that Adam will be one of the students chosen to carry papers to the office? _____

LESSON
19-3
Combinations and Probability
Practice and Problem Solving: C

For Problems 1–3, calculate the number of combinations.

1. For English class you are required to read 4 books out of a list of
   20 books. How many 4-book combinations are there?   _____
   One of the books is *To Kill a Mockingbird.* How many of the
   combinations include this book?   _____

   What fraction of the total combinations include any particular book?   _____

2. Rick & Jean's ice cream shop has 18 flavors of ice cream. How many
   3-scoop combinations are possible if the same flavor can be used for
   more than 1 scoop?   _____

3. Bree has to select 5 photos from a box containing 25 photos to use in
   the yearbook. How many different sets of 5 photos could she choose?   _____

For Problems 4–8, calculate the probabilities.

4. Jordan wants to turn on 3 lights, but he's not sure which of the
   5 switches on the panel control the lights. What is the probability
   that he will guess the correct 3 switches?   _____

   What is the probability that he will guess at least one wrong switch? _____

5. Four friends are playing a card game that uses
   16 cards—the jack, queen, king, and ace of each
   of the 4 suits. The cards are dealt out, each

Clubs	Diamonds	Hearts	Spades
♣	♦	♥	♠

   person receiving 4 cards. What is the probability
   that one person will get all 4 aces?

   Explain. _____

   _____

6. In the scenario for Problem 5, what is the probability that one person
   will get jack, queen, king, and ace of one suit?   _____

7. What is the probability that one person will get jack, queen, king, and
   ace of any suits? Explain.

   _____

   _____

8. Garrett is playing a game with a spinner that has the numbers 1–6.
   He has 3 spins left, and he needs at least two 6s in order to win.
   What are his chances of winning? Explain.

   _____

   _____

LESSON 19-4

Mutually Exclusive and Overlapping Events

Practice and Problem Solving: A/B

For Problems 1–3, answer the questions about mutually exclusive or overlapping events.

1. Are the events "choosing a black card" and "choosing a 10" from a deck of playing cards mutually exclusive? Explain why or why not.

_____

2. If there are 52 cards in a deck, with 2 red suits (groups of 13 different cards) and 2 black suits, what is the probability that a card drawn will be black and a 10? _____

3. A can of vegetables with no label has a $\frac{1}{8}$ chance of being green beans and a $\frac{1}{5}$ chance of being corn. Are the events "green beans" and "corn" mutually exclusive? _____
What is the probability that an unlabeled can of vegetables is either green beans or corn? _____

Ben spins a spinner with the numbers 1–8. For Problems 4–6, find each probability.

4. Ben spins a multiple of 3 or a multiple of 5. _____

5. Ben spins a number greater than 2 or an even number. _____

6. Ben spins a prime number or an odd number. _____

For Problems 7–10, use the scenario described below.

Of the 400 doctors who attended a conference, 240 practiced family medicine and 130 were from countries outside the United States. One-third of the family medicine practitioners were not from the United States.

	Family Medicine	Not Family Medicine	Total
From US	160		
Not From US		50	
Total			400

7. Complete the two-way table using this information.

8. What is the probability that a doctor at the conference practices family medicine or is from the United States? _____

9. What is the probability that a doctor at the conference practices family medicine or is not from the United States? _____

10. What is the probability that a doctor at the conference does not practice family medicine or is from the United States? _____

LESSON 19-4	**Mutually Exclusive and Overlapping Events**
	Practice and Problem Solving: C

Use the scenario in the box for Problems 1–3. Tell whether the events are mutually exclusive (ME) or overlapping (O), and give the probability of each.

> Cards numbered 1–25 are placed in a bag and one is drawn at random.

1. drawing an odd number or a multiple of 7 _____ $P =$ _____

2. drawing an even number or a perfect square _____ $P =$ _____

3. drawing a prime number greater than 10 or a multiple of 5 _____ $P =$ _____

Use the table and description of the experiment for Problems 4–6. Express probabilities as fractions and as decimals to the nearest hundredth.

> A drug company is testing the side effects of different doses of a new drug on three different groups of volunteers.

Group	Volunteers	Daily Amount (mg)
A	353	150
B	467	200
C	310	250

4. If a volunteer is chosen randomly, what is the probability that this person receives the highest dose of the drug per day? _____

5. If a volunteer is chosen randomly, what is the probability that this person receives more than 150 milligrams per day? _____

6. If a volunteer is chosen randomly, what is the probability that this person does **not** receive 200 milligrams per day? _____

Use the scenario in the box for Problems 7 and 8. Express probabilities as decimals.

> Mr. Rodney has 28 students in his class. Six students have blonde hair, 10 have blue eyes, and 5 have brown eyes. The blonde-haired students make up $\frac{1}{5}$ of the blue-eyed students and $\frac{3}{5}$ of the brown-eyed students.

7. What is the probability that a student in the class has blonde hair and blue eyes? _____

8. What is the probability that a student in the class has blonde hair and brown eyes? _____

Find the probabilities for Problems 9 and 10.

9. A student is collecting a population of laboratory mice to be used in an experiment. He finds that of the 236 mice in the lab, 173 mice are female and 99 have pink eyes. Just 10 of the pink-eyed mice are male. What is the probability that a mouse is female or has pink eyes? _____

10. A group of 4 friends buys a CD of 12 computer screen savers. Each friend will pick 1 screen saver to use on their computer. What is the probability that at least 2 of the friends will choose the same screen saver for their computer? _____

LESSON 20-1

Conditional Probability

Practice and Problem Solving: A/B

Use the table to find the probabilities in Problems 1–4. Write your answer as a percentage rounded to an integer.

The table shows the results of a customer satisfaction survey of 100 randomly selected shoppers at a mall. They were asked if they would shop at an earlier time if the mall opened earlier.

	Ages 10–20	Ages 21–45	Ages 46–65	65 and Older	Total
Yes	0.13	0.02	0.08	0.24	0.47
No	0.25	0.10	0.15	0.03	0.53
Total	0.38	0.12	0.23	0.27	1

1. What is the probability that a person aged 10–20 answered yes?

   _____

2. What is the probability that a person aged 65 and older answered no?

   _____

3. What is the probability that a person who answered no is aged 21–45?

   _____

4. What is the probability that a person aged 46–65 answered yes?

   _____

Find each probability. Express your answer as a percentage rounded to an integer.

5. Jerrod collected data on 100 randomly selected students. He found that 62 students owned an MP3 player, and 28 of these students also owned a smartphone. What is the probability that a person who owns an MP3 player also owns a smartphone?

   _____

6. A poll of 75 students in a class shows that 61 like chocolate ice cream. Of these, 14 also like strawberry ice cream. What is the probability that a student who likes chocolate ice cream also likes strawberry ice cream?

   _____

Name _____ Date _____ Class _____

Conditional Probability
Practice and Problem Solving: C

Use the table to find the probabilities in Problems 1–4. Write your answer as a percentage rounded to an integer.

The table shows the results of a poll of randomly selected high school students. They were asked if they think smartphones should be allowed in class.

	9th Graders	10th Graders	11th Graders	12th Graders	Total
Yes	0.15	0.16	0.19	0.18	0.68
No	0.12	0.11	0.05	0.04	0.32
Total	0.27	0.27	0.24	0.22	1

1. What is the probability that a 9th or 10th grader answered yes?

   _____

2. What is the probability that an 11th or 12th grader answered no?

   _____

3. What is the probability that a 9th or 11th grader answered yes?

   _____

4. What is the probability that a 10th or 12th grader answered no?

   _____

Solve.

5. Sarah asked 40 randomly selected students at her high school whether they were planning to go to college and whether they were planning to move out of their parents' or guardians' homes right after high school. The results are summarized in the table.

		Go to College		
		Yes	No	Total
Move Out	Yes	12	9	21
	No	8	1	9

Which is more likely, that a student planning to go to college is also planning to move out, or that a student planning to move out is also planning to go to college? Justify your response with conditional probabilities.

_____

_____

LESSON
20-2

Independent Events
Practice and Problem Solving: A/B

Find each probability.

1. Salene rolls a 1–6 number cube two times. What is the probability she will roll a 6 both times?   _____

2. Kalie rolls a 1–6 number cube two times. What is the probability she will roll an even number both times?   _____

3. Jamar rolls a 1–6 number cube three times. What is the probability he will roll an even number, then a 6, then a 4?   _____

A bag contains 4 red balls, 6 green balls, and 8 yellow balls. Find each probability for randomly removing balls with replacement.

4. removing a yellow ball two times and then a red ball   _____

5. removing a green ball, then a red ball, and then a yellow ball   _____

6. removing a green ball, then a yellow ball, then a red ball, and then a green ball   _____

For Problems 7–9, find the probability of making the spins.

7. spinning a number followed by a letter

   _____

8. spinning a 2, then a letter, then an even number

   _____

9. spinning a letter, then an odd number, then a 4

   _____

10. spinning a letter, then a 4, then a C

   _____

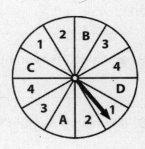

Name _____ Date _____ Class_____

Independent Events

Practice and Problem Solving: C

Find each probability.

1. In cooking class, students randomly choose 1 of 5 different recipes. Two students choose the same recipe.

    _____

2. Steven rolls a 1–6 number cube four times. The result is 4 odd numbers.

    _____

3. Beth draws four cards out of a 52-card deck with replacement. The deck has four aces. She randomly draws an ace four times.

    _____

A bag contains 4 red balls, 2 green balls, 3 yellow balls, and 5 blue balls. Find each probability for randomly removing balls with replacement.

4. removing a yellow, a red, a green, and a blue ball

    _____

5. removing a blue, a green, a green, and a yellow ball

    _____

6. removing a red, a red, a yellow, and a yellow ball

    _____

7. removing a green, a yellow, a yellow, and a red ball

    _____

Find each probability.

8. spinning a number greater than 3 and a number less than 5

    _____

9. spinning an even number and a number greater than 4

    _____

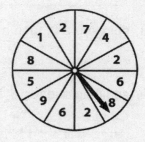

10. spinning a number less than 3 and a number greater than 3

    _____

11. spinning an odd number and a number less than 4

    _____

LESSON 20-3

Dependent Events

Practice and Problem Solving: A/B

A bag contains tiles with the letters shown at the right. Find the probability for randomly drawing tiles, one after the other, without replacing them.

1. A and then B   _____

2. C and then E   _____

3. B and then D   _____

4. E, then C, and then B _____

5. D, then A, and then A _____

A A A B
B C C D
E F G G

There are 3 apples, 4 oranges, and a pear in a bag. Determine each probability.

6. You select an orange and then a pear at random without replacement.   _____

7. You select an apple and then a pear at random without replacement.   _____

8. You select an orange, then an apple, and then a pear at random without replacement.   _____

9. You select an apple, then an orange, and then another apple without replacement.   _____

A bag contains balls with the colors shown at the right. Find the probability for randomly selecting balls, one after the other, without replacing them.

10. blue and then red   _____

11. blue and then blue   _____

12. green and then blue   _____

13. blue and then red   _____

14. red and then red   _____

15. green and then green   _____

green   green   red
red   red   red
blue   blue   blue

Dependent Events

LESSON 20-3

Practice and Problem Solving: C

The spinner shown here is spun twice.

1. The sum of the results is equal to or greater than 10, and the first spin lands on 4.

   a. Find the probability. _____

   b. Explain why the events are dependent.

   _____

2. The first spin lands on 6 and the sum of the results is less than or equal to 10.

   a. Find the probability. _____

   b. Explain why the events are dependent.

   _____

The table shows the population distribution in Ireland in 1996 by age and gender.

	Age 0–20	Age 21–40	Age 41–60	Age 61–80	Age Over 80	Total
Males (in thousands)	620.4	526.8	405.3	212.0	33.0	1797.5
Females (in thousands)	588.3	527.6	400.8	246.3	60.3	1823.3
Total	1208.7	1054.4	806.1	458.3	93.3	3620.8

Use the information in the table to find each probability.

3. A randomly selected person is no more than 20 years old, given that the person is male. _____

4. A randomly selected person is female, given that the person is over 80 years old. _____

A bag contains 3 red balls, 7 yellow balls, 5 green balls, and 3 blue balls. Find the probability of selecting these sets without replacement.

5. a red, then a blue, then a green, then a green _____

6. a blue, then a blue, then a blue, then a red _____

LESSON 21-1

Using Probability to Make Fair Decisions
Practice and Problem Solving: A/B

Determine whether the method described is a fair way to choose a winner. Explain your answer.

1. Roll a standard die. Amanda wins if the result is prime or 1. Beto wins if the result is composite.

   _____

2. Draw a card from a standard deck of 52 cards. Nicholas wins if the card is clubs or diamonds. Jake wins if the card is spades or hearts.

   _____

The student union has a prize to give to one of its volunteers. The union decides that everyone should have a chance of winning the prize based on how many hours he or she worked voluntarily. The table shows the names and number of hours worked for each volunteer. Use this information for Problems 3–4.

Volunteer	Hours Worked	Volunteer	Hours Worked
Braden	16	Mei	6
Lani	12	Pedro	4
Angel	8	Isaac	4

3. Describe a fair method that can be used to decide who wins the prize.

   _____

4. Find the percent chance of winning for each volunteer.

   _____

Sulyn and Jasmin find a box containing 40 beads. To determine who should get the beads, they toss a coin until Sulyn gets 15 heads or Jasmin gets 15 tails. Their game is cut short when Sulyn has 13 heads and Jasmin has 12 tails. Use this information for Problems 5–6.

5. What is the probability that Sulyn would have won? What is the probability that Jasmin would have won?

   _____

6. Based on the probabilities, how should the beads be divided? If there are fractional results, what would a fair method be for dividing the last bead?

   _____

Using Probability to Make Fair Decisions
Practice and Problem Solving: C

Determine whether the method described is a fair way to choose a winner. Explain your answer.

1. Roll two standard die. Shaylin wins if the sum is prime. Rachael wins if the sum is composite.

   _____

2. Draw a card from a standard deck of 52 cards. Ian wins if the card is a face card or ace. Malia wins if the card is numbered.

   _____

A charity is having a raffle at their annual fundraising event. They decide each donor family should have a chance of winning a door prize based on how many raffle tickets they purchase. The table shows the names and number of tickets purchased by each family. Use this information for Problems 3–4.

Family	Tickets Purchased	Family	Tickets Purchased
Mason	160	Lopez	25
Jackson	75	Blackwell	10
Chang	50	Sperling	5

3. Describe a fair method that can be used to decide who wins the prize.

   _____

4. Find each family's chance of winning to the nearest tenth of a percent.

   _____

Conner and Malik are twins. For their birthday, they received $40 each. They decide to play a game of chance by putting all the money in a pot. To determine who should win the pot, they toss a coin until Conner gets 25 heads or Malik gets 25 tails. Their game is interrupted when Conner has 22 heads and Malik has 19 tails. Use this information for Problems 5–6.

5. What is the probability that Conner would have won? What is the probability that Malik would have won?

   _____

6. Based on the probabilities, how should the pot be divided?

   _____

LESSON 21-2

Analyzing Decisions
Practice and Problem Solving: A/B

Rachael is giving away passes for a family fun center to adults she sees at the movies. She wants the passes to go to parents of minors. Her town has a population of 10,000 adults. Of the adults:

- 40% are not parents of minors.
- 88% who are not parents of minors go to the movies.
- 70% who are parents of minors don't go to the movies.

Use this information for Problems 1–3.

1. Complete the two-way table.

	Go to the Movies	Don't Go to the Movies	Total
Parents of Minors			
Not Parents of Minors			
Total			

2. What percent of movie-goers are parents of minors? Round to the nearest tenth of a percent.

_____

3. Do you think Rachael's decision to give passes to adults she sees at the movies is reasonable? Explain.

_____

Solve.

4. A camping supply store gets 40% of its headlamps from Company A and the remainder from Company B. The owner of the store knows that 20% of the headlamps in the last shipment from Company A were defective, while only 2% of the headlamps from Company B were defective.

a. What percent of defective headlamps come from Company B?

_____

b. What percent of defective headlamps come from Company A?

_____

c. The owner chooses a headlamp at random and finds that it is defective. She decides that the headlamp is most likely to have come from Company A. Do you think this is a reasonable conclusion? Explain.

_____

Analyzing Decisions

LESSON 21-2

Practice and Problem Solving: C

It is known that 0.8% of the population has a certain virus. A test correctly identifies people who have the virus 97% of the time. The test correctly identifies people who do not have the virus 94% of the time. Use this information for Problems 1–3.

1. Complete the two-way table. Assume a total population of 100,000 people have been tested.

	Tests Positive	Tests Negative	Total
Has the Virus			
Does Not Have the Virus			
Total			

2. Of the people who test positive for the virus, what percent actually have the virus? Round to the nearest tenth of a percent.

_____

3. A doctor recommends that anyone who tests positive for the virus should immediately start taking medication. Do you think this is a good recommendation? Explain.

_____

Solve.

4. Sal has collected data on whether the students in his school like to sleep in or exercise on weekends. The results of his study are as follows:

   • 37.5% of all students in his school like to sleep in.

   • 40% of those who sleep in also like to exercise.

   • 12% of those who don't like to sleep in also don't like to exercise.

   a. What percent of students who don't like to sleep in like to exercise?

   _____

   b. What percent of students who don't like to exercise like to sleep in?

   _____

   c. Would it be reasonable for Sal to conclude that a student who doesn't like to exercise likes to sleep in? Explain.

   _____

Data-Gathering Techniques

LESSON 22-1

Practice and Problem Solving: A/B

A school committee is planning an academic Olympics to raise money for the school. The committee surveys a random sample of 40 classrooms in which the students would need to participate as a team. The survey results show how many students in each class would be interested in participating and, if so, what subject the team prefers (math, history, or computer science) and how many of the three subjects the teams would participate in. Of the 24 classrooms surveyed, 6 indicated an interest in participating. The table lists the data for those 6 classrooms.

Preferred Subject	Number of Students Interested in Participating	Number of Academic Subjects Students Would Participate In
Math	6	1
Computer science	4	2
Math	5	1
History	9	3
History	2	2
Computer science	3	2

1. Calculate the proportion of classrooms that indicated an interest in participating. Round to the nearest thousandth.

   _____

2. Calculate the proportion of those interested in participating who prefer history. Round to the nearest thousandth.

   _____

3. If 1500 students are in the school, predict the number of students who would participate that prefer history.

   _____

4. For those with an interest in participating, calculate the mean number of classroom members who might participate and the mean number of academic subjects that those classroom members might participate in. Round to the nearest tenth.

   _____

5. If the committee receives $15 vouchers for each student who participates, predict the amount that will be raised from the events.

   _____

Data-Gathering Techniques
Practice and Problem Solving: C

A hotel chain is planning a promotional event to raise its customer base. The chain surveys a random sample of 4500 households from a community to see if adults would travel for a nominal fee in exchange for attending a promotional seminar. The survey results show how many adults in each household would be interested in participating and, if so, what location is preferred (ocean, mountains, and city) and how many of the three locations the participants would go to. Of the 27 households surveyed, 7 indicated an interest in participating. The table lists the data for those 7 households.

Preferred Location	Number of Adults Interested in Participating	Number of Locations Participants Would Go To
Ocean	2	1
Mountains	4	3
City	3	2
Mountains	1	1
City	3	1
Ocean	4	2
Ocean	2	3

1. Calculate the proportion of households that indicated an interest in participating. Round to the nearest thousandth.

_____

2. Calculate the proportion of those interested in participating who prefer traveling to the ocean. Round to the nearest thousandth.

_____

3. If approximately 11,250 adults live in the community, predict the number who would participate that prefer traveling to the ocean.

_____

4. For those with an interest in participating, calculate the mean number of household members who might participate and the mean number of locations that those household members might go to. Round to the nearest tenth.

_____

5. If the nominal fee for travel is $50 for each adult that participates, predict the amount that the hotel chain can expect from the promotion.

_____

**LESSON
22-2**

Shape, Center, and Spread
Practice and Problem Solving: A/B

Solve each problem. Round answers to two decimal places.

1. The table below shows a major league baseball player's season home
   run totals for the first 14 years of his career.

Season	1	2	3	4	5	6	7	8	9	10	11	12	13	14
Home Runs	18	22	21	28	30	29	32	40	33	34	28	29	22	20

a. Find the mean, median, standard deviation, and
   interquartile range for the data.   _____

b. Make a line plot for the data.

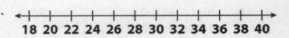

18 20 22 24 26 28 30 32 34 36 38 40

2. For three weeks, the number of calls per day to a fire and rescue
   service were recorded. The results are shown below.

Calls for Service										
5	17	2	12	0	6	3	8	15	1	4
19	16	8	2	11	13	18	3	10	6	

a. Find the mean, median, standard deviation, and
   interquartile range for the data.   _____

b. Draw a histogram for the data. Is the distribution
   symmetrical? Explain.

   _____

   _____

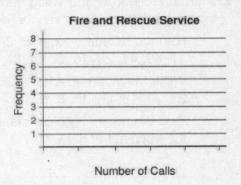

3. For 10 weeks, Kay recorded the amount of gas, in gallons, she used
   while driving. The results were 10, 14, 18, 12, 20, 24, 9, 25, 14, 16.

a. Find the mean, median, standard deviation, and
   interquartile range for the data.   _____

b. Make a box plot for the data. What type of shape
   does the box plot show? Explain.

   _____

   _____

LESSON
22-2

Shape, Center, and Spread
Practice and Problem Solving: C

Solve each problem. Round answers to two decimal places.

1. The line plot below shows the ages of 20 presidents of the United States upon first taking office.

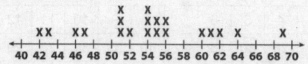

a. Find the mean, median, standard deviation, and interquartile range for the data.

_____

b. Describe the shape of the data. What does the shape tell you in terms of the problem situation?

_____

c. A president not included in the data set above is Grover Cleveland, who took office on March 4, 1893. Based on your work so far, make an educated guess as to his age that day. Explain your reasoning. Then find his age on the Internet.

_____

2. Harmon Killebrew and Willie Mays were two of baseball's greatest home run hitters. Their season home run totals are shown below.

Harmon Killebrew: 0, 4, 5, 2, 0, 42, 31, 46, 48, 45, 49, 25, 39, 44, 17, 49, 41, 28, 26, 5, 13, 14

Willie Mays: 20, 4, 41, 51, 36, 35, 29, 34, 29, 40, 49, 38, 47, 52, 37, 22, 23, 13, 28, 18, 8, 6

a. Find the mean, median, standard deviation, and interquartile range for the each set of data.

_____

b. Make a double box plot for Killebrew and Mays.

↔

c. Use the box plots to describe how Killebrew and Mays were alike and different in their home run production.

_____

Name _____ Date _____ Class_____

Probability Distributions

Practice and Problem Solving: A/B

A spinner has three equal sections, labeled 1, 2, and 3. You spin the spinner twice and find the absolute value of the difference of the two numbers the spinner lands on. Use this information for Problems 1–4.

1. Let X be a random variable that represents the absolute value of the difference of the two numbers. What are the possible values of X?

   _____

2. Fill in the table for the probability distribution.

Absolute Value of the Difference			
Probability			

3. Make a histogram of the probability distribution.

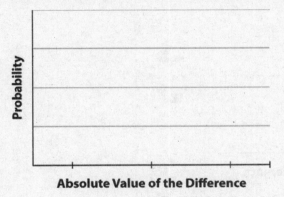

Absolute Value of the Difference

4. What is the probability that the absolute value of the difference is not 2? How is this probability represented in the histogram?

   _____

Solve.

5. Sports drinks are purchased by 3 out of 4 students using the campus snack machines. There are 3 students at the machines now. Use the formula for binomial probability, $P(r) = {}_nC_r p^r q^{n-r}$, to determine the probability that at least 2 of the students will buy a sports drink.

   _____

Probability Distributions

Practice and Problem Solving: C

A spinner has four equal sections, labeled 1, 2, 3, and 4. You spin the spinner twice and find the absolute value of the difference of the two numbers the spinner lands on. Use this information for Problems 1–4.

1. Let X be a random variable that represents the absolute value of the difference of the two numbers. What are the possible values of X?

   _____

2. Fill in the table for the probability distribution.

Absolute Value of the Difference				
Probability				

3. Make a histogram of the probability distribution.

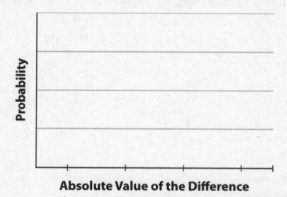

Absolute Value of the Difference

4. What is the probability that the absolute value of the difference is not 1? How is this probability represented in the histogram?

   _____

Solve.

5. Sales records for the snack machines show that 1 out of every 6 students buys a bag of trail mix. There are 5 students waiting to use the machines.

   a. What is the probability of exactly 3 students buying a bag of trail mix?

   _____

   b. What is the probability of at least 1 student buying a bag of trail mix?

   _____

LESSON 23-2

Normal Distributions

Practice and Problem Solving: A/B

At a shoe factory, the number of various shoe sizes produced is normally distributed with a mean of size 9 and a standard deviation of 1.5 sizes. Use this information for Problems 1–3.

1. What is the probability that a shoe size will be larger than size 10.5 if a supervisor chooses a shoe at random?

   _____

2. What is the probability that a shoe size will be smaller than size 6 if a supervisor chooses a shoe at random?

   _____

3. What is the probability that a shoe size will be between sizes 7.5 and 12 if a supervisor chooses a shoe at random?

   _____

Scores on a test are normally distributed with a mean of 78 and a standard deviation of 8. Use the table below to find each probability.

z	−2.5	−2	−1.5	−1	−0.5	0	0.5	1	1.5	2	2.5
Area	0.01	0.02	0.07	0.16	0.31	0.5	0.69	0.84	0.93	0.98	0.99

4. A randomly selected student scored below 90. _____

5. A randomly selected student scored above 86. _____

6. A randomly selected student scored between 86 and 90. _____

7. A randomly selected student scored between 74 and 78. _____

Solve.

8. The ages of 20 people who sing in the choir are given below. If the mean of all the ages of the people in the choir is 40 years and the standard deviation is 12 years, do the data appear to be normally distributed? Explain.

25	37	32	38	51
62	52	54	29	35
39	58	30	28	34
34	36	37	64	25

LESSON 23-2

Normal Distributions

Practice and Problem Solving: C

The stride lengths, in feet, in a group of adult males are normally distributed with a mean of 2.5 feet and a standard deviation of 0.04 feet. Use this information for Problems 1–3.

1. What is the probability that the stride length of a randomly selected adult male is less than 2.58 feet?

   _____

2. What is the probability that the stride length of a randomly selected adult male is between 2.38 feet and 2.46 feet?

   _____

3. What is the probability that the stride length of a randomly selected adult male is between 2.42 feet and 2.54 feet?

   _____

Scores on a test are normally distributed with a mean of 81.2 and a standard deviation of 3.6. Use the table below to find each probability.

z	−2.5	−2	−1.5	−1	−0.5	0	0.5	1	1.5	2	2.5
Area	0.01	0.02	0.07	0.16	0.31	0.5	0.69	0.84	0.93	0.98	0.99

4. A randomly selected student scored below 74. _____

5. A randomly selected student scored above 88.4. _____

6. A randomly selected student scored between 81.2 and 84.8. _____

7. A randomly selected student scored between 77.6 and 88.4. _____

Solve.

8. The stride lengths, in feet, in a group of adult females are given below. If standard deviation in the stride lengths is 0.02 ft, do the data appear to be normally distributed? Explain.

1.78	1.85	1.87	1.96	2.02
2.04	2.05	2.05	2.17	2.19
2.23	2.25	2.26	2.28	2.35
2.38	2.41	2.43	2.55	2.68

Sampling Distributions

LESSON 23-3

Practice and Problem Solving: A/B

A study showed that the mean age of visitors at a large art museum is 42 years old with a standard deviation of 6.2 years. You choose a random sample of 25 visitors. Use this information for Problems 1–4.

1. Find the mean of the sampling distribution of the sample mean.

   _____

2. Find the standard error of the mean.

   _____

3. What interval captures 95% of the means for random samples of 25 visitors?

   _____

4. What is the probability that your sample has a mean age of at most 45 years?

   _____

About 38% of students at a large school play an instrument. Chelsea chooses a random sample of 70 students at the school. Use this information for Problems 5–9.

5. Find the mean of the sampling distribution of the sample proportion.

   _____

6. Find the standard error of the proportion.

   _____

7. What is the probability that Chelsea's sample has more than 25 students who play an instrument?

   _____

8. What is the probability that Chelsea's sample has a proportion between 25% and 35%?

   _____

9. Find the interval that captures 68% of the proportions for random samples of 70 students.

   _____

**LESSON
23-3**

Sampling Distributions
Practice and Problem Solving: C

**The meanlength of songs played by a radio station is 3.7 minutes with
a standard deviation of 1.3 minutes. The station chooses a random
sample of 30 songs. Use this information for Problems 1–5.**

1. Find the mean of the sampling distribution of the sample mean.

   _____

2. Find the standard error of the mean.

   _____

3. What interval captures 99.7% of the means for random samples of
   30 songs?

   _____

4. What is the probability that the sample has a mean songlength
   between 3 and 3.5 minutes?

   _____

5. What is the probability that the total airtime of the 30 randomly
   selected songs exceeds 126 minutes?

   _____

**About 23 out of every 100 students at Rafael's high school have a
blog. Rafael chooses a random sample of 85 students at his high
school. Use this information for Problems 6–9.**

6. Find the mean of the sampling distribution of the sample proportion.

   _____

7. Find the standard error of the proportion.

   _____

8. What is the probability that Rafael's sample has at most 17 students
   who have a blog?

   _____

9. What is the probability that Rafael's sample has between 20 and 30
   students who have a blog?

   _____

Name _____ Date _____ Class_____

Confidence Intervals and Margins of Error
Practice and Problem Solving: A/B

Find the confidence interval for the proportion or the mean in each situation. Round to two decimal places.

1. Rachael surveys a random sample of 80 students at her high school and finds that 18 of the students have a part-time job. Find a 90% confidence interval for the proportion p of students at Rachael's school who have a part-time job.

_____

2. A quality control team of a light bulb manufacturer measures the life of 125 randomly selected incandescent bulbs and finds that the mean amount of bulb life is 1600 hours. Given that the population standard deviation is 200 hours, find a 99% confidence interval for the mean amount of incandescent bulb life.

_____

Find the appropriate sample size for each situation. Round to the nearest whole number.

3. The marketing department of an internet radio station wants to know the percent of residents in a large state who listen to internet radio. Based on data from other states, they estimate $\hat{p} = 0.62$. They are aiming for a 95% confidence interval and a margin of error of 4%. How many state residents should they survey?

_____

4. Henry owns a sport supply store and wants to know the mean amount of revenue per week. He is aiming for a 90% confidence interval and a margin of error of $200. Given that the population standard deviation is $600, what sample size should Henry use?

_____

Solve. Round to three decimal places.

5. A group of researchers from a major health organization surveys a random sample of 435 adult residents of a state to find the percent of people who get a check-up at least once a year. Suppose the proportion p of the population who get a check-up at least once a year is 28.3%. What are the reasonably likely values of $\hat{p}$ that fall within 2 standard deviations of p?

_____

Name _____ Date _____ Class_____

Confidence Intervals and Margins of Error
Practice and Problem Solving: C

Find the confidence interval for the proportion or the mean in each situation. Round to two decimal places.

1. In a random sample of 1625 families from a large state, approximately 273 of the families travel at least 300 miles away from home once or more each year. Find a 95% confidence interval for the proportion p of families in the state that travel at least 300 miles away from home once or more each year.

_____

2. Garrett surveys 184 randomly selected residents in his city and finds that the mean amount of time spent watching television per week is 14 hours, 45 minutes. Given that the population standard deviation is 42 minutes, find a 90% confidence interval for the mean amount of hours residents of Garrett's city spend watching television per week.

_____

Find the appropriate sample size for each situation. Round to the nearest whole number.

3. A researcher wants to know the percent of adults with bank accounts in the United States that do all or most of their banking online. Based on a similar recent study, he estimates $\hat{p} = 0.25$. He is aiming for a 99% confidence interval and a margin of error of 2.25%. How many adults with bank accounts should the researcher survey?

_____

4. Charlene manages the marketing division of a tent manufacturing company and wants to know the mean number of minutes it takes customers to assemble a two-man tent. She is aiming for a 95% confidence interval and a margin of error of 0.25 minutes. Through past experience, Charlene knows that the population standard deviation is 1.3 minutes. What sample size should Charlene use?

_____

Solve. Round to three decimal places.

5. A research group surveys a random sample of 675 teenagers in a state to find the percent of teens that eat vegetables less than once daily. Suppose the proportion p of the population who eat vegetables less than once daily is 33.2%. What are the reasonably likely values of $\hat{p}$ that fall within 2 standard deviations of p?

_____

LESSON 24-2

Surveys, Experiments, and Observational Studies

Practice and Problem Solving: A/B

Explain whether each situation is an experiment or an observational study.

1. A teacher asks her students to write down everything they eat in a day and then calculate the total number of calories consumed.

   _____

2. A marine biologist visits a certain beach in Florida every year and counts the number of eggs in sea turtle nests.

   _____

3. The cafeteria manager of a high school wants to find out if high prices are keeping students from using the cafeteria. Fifty students are chosen at random to receive half-price lunch passes every day for a month. The manager then records the number of passes used.

   _____

The studies described below are randomized comparative experiments. Describe the treatment, the characteristic of interest, the treatment group, and the control group.

4. A medical researcher collects data about a certain medicine. She asks 10 patients to take the medicine and another 10 patients to take a placebo (a sugar pill known to have no effect). None of the patients knows which group he or she is in. At the end of six months, the group taking the medicine showed more improvement in its symptoms than the group taking the placebo.

   _____

5. A department store wants to increase its sales. It assembled 100 of its best credit card customers and randomly divided them into two groups of 50. One group was allowed to use a special website for ordering goods and paying bills and the other group was not. At the end of six months, the group using the special website made 40% more purchases than the other group.

   _____

Explain whether the research topic is best addressed through an experiment or an observational study. Then explain how you would set up the experiment or observational study.

6. Does getting less than 7 hours of sleep per night affect how students perform in their morning classes?

   _____

   _____

7. Do people who take zinc as a dietary supplement each day have fewer colds than people who do not take zinc supplements?

   _____

   _____

LESSON 24-2 Surveys, Experiments, and Observational Studies
Practice and Problem Solving: C

Explain whether each situation is an experiment or an observational study.

1. A school guidance counselor wants to know whether students with older siblings who went away to college are more likely to want to go away to college themselves. She interviews students about whether they have older siblings who went away to college and whether they are planning to themselves.

_____

2. The manager of a grocery store wants to know if a product's location in the store affects how well the product sells. He first tracks how many of a certain item sells over a month when the display is located where it always has been. He then moves the display to the front of the store so that customers see it when they first enter. He again tracks how many of the items sell over a month and compares the numbers.

_____

3. A researcher wants to know whether teens in warmer climates tend to be more physically active than teens in colder climates. She randomly selects 100 teens in states with typically colder climates and 100 teens in 3 states with typically warmer climates and surveys them all about their levels of activity.

_____

The studies described below are randomized comparative experiments. Describe the treatment, the characteristic of interest, the treatment group, and the control group.

4. A researcher wants to know whether background noise affects people's abilities to complete simple cognitive tasks. She has 20 people perform a series of tasks. Ten randomly selected subjects perform the tasks in a quiet room. The other 10 perform the tasks in a room that has traffic noise outside and muffled voices coming from the room next door. She records how successful each group of subjects is in completing the assigned tasks.

_____

5. The members of a transportation department in a city are deciding whether it will save them money in the long run to use a new, more expensive asphalt mixture to pave their roads. Of 6 city roads scheduled for repaving, they pave 3 with the new asphalt and 3 with the old asphalt. After one year's wear, they study the conditions of the roads.

_____

Explain whether the research topic is best addressed through an experiment or an observational study. Then explain how you would set up the experiment or observational study.

6. Will offering access to internet-equipped computers to non-members of a library increase the number of new members?

_____

_____

_____

Determining the Significance of Experimental Results

LESSON 24-3

Practice and Problem Solving: A/B

Mr. Kaplan is supervising an experiment in his science class in order to find out whether adding salt to water causes the water to boil more quickly. Each student in the class records how long it takes his or her beaker of water to boil when placed on a burner. Half of the students do not add salt to the water and half of the students add a teaspoon of salt to the water. The results of the experiment, in seconds, are shown below. Use this information for Problems 1–2.

Control	65	78	62	71	73
Treatment	63	70	74	68	69

1. State the null hypothesis for the experiment.

_____

2. Calculate the mean of the control group, $\bar{x}_C$, and the treatment group, $\bar{x}_T$. Does the result of the experiment appear to be statistically significant?

_____

A research team is testing whether a fuel additive has a significant effect on a car's gas mileage. The gas mileage, in miles per gallon (mpg), of a certain make and model of car is known to have a mean mileage of 22.4 mpg. A random sample of that model car was given the treatment. The result was a mean mileage of 26.7 mpg. Use this information for Problems 3–6.

3. State the null hypothesis for the experiment.

_____

4. State the mean mileage for the treatment group, $\bar{x}_T$, and the mean mileage for the control group, $\bar{x}_C$. Then find the difference of the means.

_____

5. Given that the null hypothesis is true, the sampling distribution for the difference of mileage is normal with a mean of 0 and a standard error of 1.9. What interval captures 95% of the differences of means in the sampling distribution?

_____

6. Determine whether the result is statistically significant, and state a conclusion about whether the null hypothesis should be rejected.

_____

LESSON 24-3
Determining the Significance of Experimental Results
Practice and Problem Solving: C

A school is testing whether a new curriculum is successful in raising final exam scores. The data show the scores of the classes that were taught with the new curriculum and the classes that continued to use the old curriculum. Use this information for Problems 1–2.

Control	72	85	72	73	90	64	75	81	70
Treatment	97	88	82	90	79	83	99	82	86

1. State the null hypothesis for the experiment.

   _____

2. Calculate the mean of the control group $\overline{x}_C$ and the treatment group $\overline{x}_T$. Does the result of the experiment appear to be statistically significant?

   _____

GoBo Toy Company manufactures rubber balls. GoBo claims its new rubber will cause its balls to bounce significantly higher than the balls made of its old rubber. In an experiment, bounce heights were measured from random samples of balls made of the old rubber and the new rubber. The balls made of the old rubber had a mean bounce height of 137.16 centimeters. The balls made of the new rubber had a mean bounce height of 149.35 centimeters. Use this information for Problems 3–6.

3. State the null hypothesis for the experiment.

   _____

4. State the mean bounce height for the treatment group $\overline{x}_T$ and the mean bounce height for the control group $\overline{x}_C$. Then find the difference of the means.

   _____

5. Given that the null hypothesis is true, the resampling distribution for the difference in bounce heights is normal with a mean of 0 and a standard error of 5.78. What interval captures 95% of the differences of means in the resampling distribution?

   _____

6. Determine whether the result is statistically significant, and state a conclusion about whether the null hypothesis should be rejected.

   _____